Four Quarters

A Cultural and Developmental Approach to Transforming Your Spiritual Autobiography

by

Taunya Marie Tinsley, D.Min., Ph.D.

Foreword by

Dr. William H. Curtis
Pastor, Mount Ararat Baptist Church

The contents of this work, including, but not limited to, the accuracy of events, people, and places depicted; opinions expressed; permission to use previously published materials included; and any advice given or actions advocated are solely the responsibility of the author, who assumes all liability for said work and indemnifies the publisher against any claims stemming from publication of the work.

All Rights Reserved
Copyright © 2020 by Taunya Marie Tinsley, D.Min., Ph.D.

No part of this book may be reproduced or transmitted, downloaded, distributed, reverse engineered, or stored in or introduced into any information storage and retrieval system, in any form or by any means, including photocopying and recording, whether electronic or mechanical, now known or hereinafter invented without permission in writing from the publisher.

Dorrance Publishing Co
585 Alpha Drive
Suite 103
Pittsburgh, PA 15238
Visit our website at www.dorrancebookstore.com

ISBN: 978-1-6442-6352-5
eISBN: 978-1-6442-6991-6

ENDORSEMENTS

Four Quarters is a quick read, but Dr. Taunya slows you down enough to HONESTLY reflect, review, renew and realize God's purpose for your life, without sitting in front of her. God is AMAZING and I'm thankful for him using her to bless me at the right time and moment.

Karmyn Jefferson,
Mark Anthony Hair Salon,
Pittsburgh, PA

*

It was a wise writer who once declared, "Regardless of how you feel inside, always try to look like a winner. Even if you are behind, a sustained look of control and confidence can give you a mental edge that results in victory." In this book Dr. Taunya Tinsley gives us colorful inspiration, illumination, and revelation, to elevate our perception about God, ourselves, and the world of athletics around us. This book is an absolute flawless work, designed to motivate the person who has allowed complacency, routine, and passion-less purpose to dominate their life.

This book will remind you why God built you to be in the game, while giving you fundamental principles that are necessary for you to stay motivated to win. This is a must read, and I highly recommend this book.

Bishop Sir Walter Mack, Jr,
Union Baptist Church,
Winston-Salem, North Carolina

Author of: *Passion For Your Kingdom Purpose, Destined For Promotion, How To Make A Wrong Relationship Right,* and *Hope For Hip Hop*

*

Dr. Taunya Tinsley presents an approach to writing one's spiritual autobiography that is unique and skillful, technical and artful. She strategically utilizes her expertise in the field of psychology, counseling, and ministry; along with her knowledge and experience as an athlete, that makes this book a powerful tool to help one look deeply into their own life experience to discover and interpret aspects of their personal story that can be life-changing. Dr. Tinsley's bold transparency challenges the reader to embrace their own truth and experience to become aware of how God works through difficult and painful experiences to shape and empower our lives.

Four Quarters is for anyone who is serious about writing a comprehensive spiritual autobiography.

Rev. Dr. Joan B. Prentice, Founder, Executive Director and Pastor of The Ephesus Project, Pittsburgh, Pennsylvania

*

The process of development is multifaceted. The approach is uniquely based upon the context of the observer and instructor and can be shaped differently or cohesively. The context is often the most overlooked portion of developed history and current settings missed and overlooked by the student. The instructor's role is to approach each student individually and uniquely, by peeling off the layers of their past, to expose the current landscape that exist in an effort to understand all the past, present and possibly future unforetold realities. This book Four Quarters does so, with carefully directed simplicity. Dr. Tinsley has used a metaphoric and an analogistic method to allow those who may or may not be athletes to create a revelation of where they may be presently, and more importantly, how they arrived. The framework of the athletic arena's time frame is used eloquently and gives a sublime view into the stark reality of life. She exposes some of her own experiences in an effort to push the student to not be hesitant in helping to make themselves whole and by doing so envelops the reader into a sense needed response. This book is a must read for every scholar and student seeking to understand how they arrived where they are today. It's a necessary read for those desiring to understand how they've been shaped and molded, whether that be good or bad. This book is a well written developmental model that sets the stage for wholeness and understanding. Its ability to make the reader self examine, creates a systematic paradigm the allows one to constantly return and seek genuine understanding of identity and self!

Dr. Robert Jackson III, Pastor,
St. Paul AME Church, Miami, FL

FOUR QUARTERS

Abstract

This book is designed to assist you with developing a personal narrative of your life through the lens of the spiritual highlighting the activity of God. The spiritual autobiography will be divided into age-based developmental periods within *four quarters* and *an overtime* that includes a description of each period, an account in which the presence of God was especially vivid and/or challenging, an overview of the crises of faith (i.e., points of crises and God's presence at those points) that were experienced, and the outcomes of growth that the crises stimulated (i.e., how the crises have affected you). The author provides examples from her personal experiences designed to assist you with identifying your spiritual story. From identifying your spiritual story and writing your spiritual autobiography utilizing journal writing prompts, your life as well as your service in the community or ministry will be transformed. Additionally, you will also be able to provide an overview of who you are today and who you are becoming. Finally, you will develop implications of how crises of faith influence and impacts you personally, professionally, and ministerially. In telling your story within this spiritual autobiography, the focus will be on the role of God in your life.

    This book is designed for anyone who is in service to others and is seeking understanding of their spiritual story to dynamically transform past experiences into new beginnings. This book can be used in a variety of settings including small groups, churches and spiritual leadership teams, seminaries, and academic programs seeking to assist their leaders, congregants, or students with identifying their spiritual story from a cultural and developmental approach. If helping professionals and those in service in the community or church are to promote growth and change in those they help, they must be willing to promote growth in their own lives.

DEDICATION

This book is dedicated to all of my clients, past, present, and future. Proverbs 27:17 (NIV) states: "As iron sharpens iron, so one man [or woman] sharpens [and influences] another [through discussion]." As we are all unique individuals due to the choices we make, we are all constantly remaking and transforming ourselves. Thank you for allowing me to be on the journey with you. Remember, *trust the process!*

CONTENTS

FOREWORD xiii

PREFACE xv

PRE-GAME 1

FIRST QUARTER 5
   Infancy/Early Childhood (Conception/Birth -12) 7
   My Spiritual Story – First Quarter .23
   Your Spiritual Story – First Quarter 31

SECOND QUARTER 35
   Adolescence (12-18) 37
   My Spiritual Story – Second Quarter 45
   Your Spiritual Story – Second Quarter 51

HALFTIME 55

THIRD QUARTER 61
   Early Adulthood (18-30) 63
   My Spiritual Story – Third Quarter 69
   Your Spiritual Story – Third Quarter 75

FOURTH QUARTER 79
   Middle Adulthood (30-60) 81

My Spiritual Story – Fourth Quarter .87
Your Spiritual Story – Fourth Quarter 93

OVERTIME 97
Older Adulthood (60-Death) 99
My Budding Spiritual Story – Overtime 105
Your Spiritual Story – Overtime 109

POST-GAME 113

PLAYBOOK SPIRITUAL AUTOBIOGRAPHY COMPONENTS . . .119
Bibliography 121
About the Author 125

FOREWORD

I met Dr. Tinsley walking across the campus of the Carnegie Mellon University on my way to speak for a student MLK Day and knew then that one day she would be offering her transparent streams of insights about the wonder of journeying with God. Academic degrees later and life experiences in tow, she carries the veterans' mantle and has logged enough time on the court we call life to write her reflections.

STORY is powerful and images build bridges and seeing one's journey through the basketball image of four quarters provides an appropriate way of dealing with discoveries, shifts, excitements, exhaustions, epiphanies, etc., that come with maturing in faith. Dr. Tinsley, having played college ball, understands the parallels between walking by faith with God and enduring four quarters on the court better than most. Both her theological and therapy background provide a fascinating bridge between two disciplines often at odds. However, if one can "play" all four quarters, it becomes evident how connected the two are. Regardless of what quarter you're in, get in the game and walk by faith on this exciting journey called "Life with God."

I suspect one of the best biblical examples of a "Hall of Fame" fourth-quarter giant is David. His reflection is why you want to read this book:

Psalm 37:25: David provides this fourth-quarter commentary:

"I have been young, and now am old;
Yet I have not seen the righteous forsaken,
Nor his descendants begging bread."

Dr. William H. Curtis
Pastor
Mount Ararat Baptist Church

PREFACE

"I believe that God made me for a purpose for China. He also made me fast, and when I run, I feel his pleasure. To give it up would be to hold Him in contempt. To win is to honor him."

Eric Liddell, *Chariots of Fire*[1]

"Sport permeates all aspects of society; that is even a person with very little interest in sport will interact with it in some way."[2] Additionally, sports are so ingrained in the social and cultural life of society that it has become a reflection of American society and an inherent component of the national cultural identity.[3] These statements describe the state of affairs with, and for the meaning of sports for over 2000 years ago.

In the New Testament, Paul structures some of his letters utilizing analogies of athletic metaphors, such as running and boxing, to illustrate the important matter of love and service over dogmatic

---

[1] Hudson, Hugh; Colin Welland; and David Puttnam. 1981. *Chariots of Fire*. London: Enigma Productions.

[2] Adrienne Leslie-Toogood. "Introduction." In *Advising Student-Athletes: A Collaborative Approach to Success (Monograph Series Number 18)*, edited by Adrienne Leslie-Toogood and Emmett Gill (Manhattan, KS: NACADA, 2008), pp. 7-12.

[3] Gary Sailes and Louis Harrison. "Social Issues of Sport." In *Advising Student-Athletes: A Collaborative Approach to Success (Monograph Series Number 18)*, edited by Adrienne Leslie-Toogood and Emmett Gill (Manhattan, KS: NACADA, 2008), pp. 13-22.

doctrinal attitudes. His analogies are designed to encourage people to value lost souls more than valuing one's own rights. Paul's athletic metaphors resonated with both the Gentile and Jewish audiences of his day. Victor Pfitzner states, "They were so general in their lack of concrete details that it is not hard to imagine that any Hellenistic Jew could have written or understood them without having gained a firsthand knowledge of the games from a bench in the stadium." The Isthmian Games, one of the major Panhellenic Games of Ancient Greece, inspired Paul's use of athletic imagery specifically for the congregants in Corinth. Richard Hays states, "They would find Paul's depictions of the athletes (i.e., the runner and the boxer) familiar, vivid, and compelling." Paul's use of athletic imagery made the gospel relevant for the culture of his day, while simultaneously subverting the secular world's values to promote the gospel, which made him a multicultural competent religious leader.

Actually, both Jesus and Paul in their historical contexts were multicultural competent religious leaders, prophets, ministers, counselors and teachers. As a multicultural competent church leader, it is important that individuals gain self-awareness and worldview knowledge as well as utilize culturally appropriate skills and interventions while having the ability to develop cross-cultural relationships.[4] Individuals should be aware of their attitudes, values and beliefs as well as understand who they are as cultural beings. Additionally, it is important that they are knowledgeable of the culture of their congregants, clients and other individuals in which they serve locally, nationally and/or globally, including their historical, socio, and political factors that contribute to, and influence devel-

---

[4] Ratts, M. J., Singh, A. A., Nassar-McMillan, S., Butler, S. K., & McCullough, J. R. (2015). *Multicultural and social justice counseling competencies*. Retrieved from https://www.counseling.org/docs/default-source/competencies/multicultural-and-social-justice-counseling-competencies.pdf?sfvrsn=8573422c_20

opment and daily functioning. It is also important that the church leader or other helping professional utilize culturally appropriate skills, techniques, language, interventions, etc., with the individuals they serve while being able to develop cross-cultural relationships.

The Church is responsible for shaping culture in the society in which they serve. "If man is to be reached, he must be reached within his own culture."[5] God became a man in the form of Jesus to come to earth and incarnate the gospel. As members of the body of Christ, we as Christian leaders must also learn to exegete ourselves, the surrounding culture and the cultural context to reach people developmentally with the gospel message. And, the Church must continue to engage in social justice and social change that reconciles brokenness with God, with self, with others, and with creation back towards peace and harmonious relationships.

As a member of the Church, whether inside the mortar brick walls of the Church or outside the four mortar brick walls of the Church in the community, it is important for each of us to engage on the journey of becoming a multicultural competent leader just as Paul and Jesus. Remember, church is where two or three gather in His name whether inside a physical building our outside (Matthew 18:20). The first step is to gain, as well as increase, your awareness of self. Who are you as a cultural being? What are your attitudes, values, and belief and where did they come from?

Just as Paul utilized analogies and metaphors from athletics in his letters, I too am inspired to utilize analogies and metaphors specifically from the sport of basketball to assist you with identifying your spiritual story. Each chapter of this book has been framed utilizing metaphors and analogies from sports, specifically basketball, to help you identify areas within the "game of your life" for the purpose of developing your spiritual autobiography. It is my hope

---

[5] George W. Peters, *A Biblical Theology of Missions* (Chicago, IL: Moody Press, 1984), p. 163.

that by journeying through your spiritual story, you will be transformed personally, professionally and ministerially.

During the *Pre-Game*, you will learn more about a spiritual autobiography and its purpose. Each age-based development period or *Quarter* as well as an *Overtime* begins with a quote or theme from the movie *Brown Sugar*[6] that includes replacing the word and concept of *Hip-Hop* to that of *basketball*. I will then briefly describe specific lifespan human development theories and social and cultural perspectives pertinent for each quarter. I specifically focused on psychosocial and cognitive theories that may assist you with understanding identity development from birth to death. Additionally, throughout this book, we will call a *Time-Out*, or a halt in the play (i.e., reading). These time-outs are called strategically at points for you to begin the reflection process of your own spiritual story.

To assist you with identifying your spiritual story, I then share snippets of my spiritual story from each *Quarter* that forms my spiritual autobiography. Additionally, within each *Quarter, Time-Outs,* and *Overtime*, you have an opportunity to reflect and identify the following:

- Your crisis points of faith that were experienced during that time period,
- God's presence at those points, and
- The outcomes of growth that the crisis stimulated.

This book would not have been possible without the Lord my God, who called me to counsel, teach, and lead for traditional and untraditional ministry. As part of my call to ministry, I had to find more out about myself within my contexts (i.e., church, community, occupational) by writing a spiritual autobiography. This was part of my Doctor of Ministry program at United Theological Seminary, Dayton, OH, and I thought it would be easy and simple due to my

---

[6] Twentieth Century Fox Film Corporation, 2002.

training as a professional counselor and counselor educator. The assignment turned out to be more challenging as I completed some unfinished business as it relates to my previous life experiences that had unbeknownst to me contributed to my development both personally, professionally, and as a Christian leader.

This transformational experience allowed me to identify and evaluate my strengths and God's use of my life's circumstances at a deeper level for the benefit of my personal, professional and ministerial development. I am a true believer that God will allow you to go through life's experiences, whether good, bad, or ugly, heal you, then place you back in those contexts to minister, teach, mentor, and/or counsel others. I am thankful for United Theological Seminary for requiring this assignment as part of our training.

I am also thankful for Dr. William H. Curtis, Senior Pastor, Mount Ararat Baptist Church, Pittsburgh, PA; Dr. Joan Prentice, Executive Director, Ephesus Project; and Dr. Chad A. White, Senior Pastor, Mt. Carmel Missionary Baptist Church, Dayton, OH, for being on the journey with me as I identified my spiritual story, and assisting me with managing the pain and tension that resulted from the process. My mentors kept me from abruptly and prematurely terminating God's ordained process for development.

I hope that as you journey through this process, you do not do it alone. We are designed to be in relationships with others. Trust the process. Additionally, it is my hope that you don't prematurely or abruptly terminate God's ordained process for you to identify your spiritual story and transform your spiritual autobiography. It's not by accident that you have this book in your hand and have read this far! I look forward to hearing about your transformative process!

Taunya Marie Tinsley, D.Min., Ph.D., NCC, LPC

PRE-GAME

Lord, you have examined me. You know me. You know when I sit down and when I stand up. Even from far away, you comprehend my plans. You study my traveling and resting. You are thoroughly familiar with all my ways. There isn't a word on my tongue, Lord, that you don't already know completely. You surround me – front and back. You put your hand on me. That kind of knowledge is too much for me; it's so high above me that I can't fathom it. Where could I go to get away from your spirit? Where could I go to escape your presence? If I went up to heaven, you would be there. If I went down to the grave, you would be there too! If I could fly on the wings of dawn, stopping to rest only on the far side of the ocean – even there your hand would guide me; even there your strong hand would hold me tight! If I said, "The darkness will definitely hide me; the light will become night around me," even then the darkness isn't too dark for you! Nighttime would shine bright as day because darkness is the same as light to you! You are the one who created my innermost parts; you knit me together while I was still in my mother's womb. I give thanks to you that I was marvelously set apart. Your works are wonderful – I know that very well. My bones weren't hidden from you when I was being put together in a secret place, when I was being woven together in the deep parts of the earth. Your eyes saw my embryo, and on your scroll every day was written that was being formed for me, before any one of them had yet happened.

God your plans are incomprehensible to me! Their total number is countless! If I tried to count them – they outnumber grains of sand! If I came to the very end – I'd still be with you. (Psalm 139: 1-18 (CEB))

A spiritual autobiography is the story of significant events, people and places that have influenced your relationship with nature, a higher power, God, spirituality, or religion. Specifically, as it relates to God, a spiritual autobiography is the story of God's interaction in your life. A spiritual autobiography chronicles your pilgrimage as you seek to follow God.[7] Reflection on your life in the context of how God has been active (and currently active) may reveal patterns and directions that were not evident at the conscious awareness level. That is, a "persistent refusal to hear and heed the Voice reduces it to a mere whisper and relegates it to the background of many lives."[8] A spiritual autobiography is not meant to be a comprehensive chronicle of your spiritual journey, but rather a selective reflection on events, periods, influences, people and experiences that you are led to write about. A spiritual autobiography is meant to draw the strands of your life together in a way that points you to their meaning; it reminds you of where true reality lies in contrast to the illusions of modern life. A spiritual autobiography encourages you to notice God's footprints, and as you notice your life is changed, you understand a new level of God's intention your life.[9]

This book is designed to assist you with developing a personal narrative of your life through the lens of the spiritual—highlighting the activity of God. The spiritual autobiography will be divided into age-based developmental periods within *Four Quarters* and an *Over-*

---

[7] Richard Peace, *Spiritual Autobiography, Discovering and Sharing Your Spiritual Story* (Colorado Springs, CO: NavPress, 1998), pp. 57-63.

[8] Peace, 57-63.

[9] Peace, 57-63.

time that includes a description of each period, an account in which the presence of God was especially vivid and/or challenging, an overview of the crises of faith (i.e., points of crises and God's presence at those points) that were experienced, and the outcomes of growth that the crises stimulated (i.e., how the crises have affected me).

From identifying your spiritual story and writing your spiritual autobiography, you will also be able to provide an overview of who you are today as well as an overview of who you are becoming. Finally, you will develop implications of how the crisis of faith influences and impacts your model of ministry. In telling your story within this spiritual autobiography, the focus will be on the role of God in your life.

Within each *Quarter* of the "game of life" including *Half-Time* and the *Post-Game,* as well as during *Time-Outs,* you will be guided to write a personal narrative of your spiritual and/or religious journey by responding to selected questions. These questions are designed to guide your writing, but should not preclude you from including other relevant material. A spiritual autobiography should demonstrate careful reflection, over a period of weeks, on your own faith, spiritual and/or religious development process. By the time you have identified your spiritual story and completed your spiritual autobiography, you will have done quite a bit of reading as well, and can make connections to ideas that have sparked reflection or memory for you.

> **'For I know the Plans and thoughts**
> **that I have for you,' says the Lord,**
> **'plans for peace and wellbeing and not**
> **for disaster to give you a future and a hope.'**
>
> **(Jeremiah 29:11 (AMP))**

FIRST QUARTER

INFANCY/EARLY CHILDHOOD
(Conception/Birth -12)

Basketball, you the love of my life!

In the movie *Brown Sugar,* a key question that is asked throughout the movie is, "So, when did you fall in love with Hip-Hop?" Because I am relating my life to basketball, the appropriate question is "So, when did you fall in love with basketball?" I remember the exact day I fell in love with basketball. It was September 4, 1967. The day I saw my mom, my birth father, my maternal grandfather, my maternal grandmother and my paternal grandmother "battle" in Urbana, Illinois, is the day I truly met basketball. Little did I know a few years later, my birth father would join his "other" significant mate and begin his life in Denver, Colorado. And of course, the "other little ones" (i.e., my birth father's other two children, my older brother by five months and my younger brother by five months) would move a couple of years later joining him for that "ideal" traditional family. Little did I know how much basketball would be a part of my life.

> Basketball was as young, naïve, confused sometimes innocent and sometimes mischievous as I was. And as I grew up, basketball grew with me and along the way it took on all my baggage, my dreams. I felt basketball and basketball felt me.

Four Quarters

And I know everyone who loves the sport feels the same way I do.

—Brown Sugar[1]

For many people, basketball was that first friend. The first to talk to us. The first to understand. Basketball has always been that kind of friend to me. And like any relationship, I watched it grow, I watched it change.

—Brown Sugar

Description of the First Quarter

Following birth, infants possess a surprising range of abilities. They have well-developed senses of touch, hearing, and smell. They can also communicate their needs by crying. During their first year, they develop many other abilities, including smiling, making vocal sounds, and babbling. By six months, infants have also learned to sit and are starting to crawl. By twelve months, infants may be saying their first words. They usually can stand with help and may even have started to walk to begin exploring the world around them.

This exploration allows for the child to learn from their experience and learn from the connections between seeing and hearing, to tell the difference between Mom's face and that of someone else, to discover that their actions have consequences, and to pay attention to the sounds emphasized in language being heard. That is, babies' and young children's language development is strongly influenced by the language they hear spoken around them and to

---

[1] The theme for my introduction for each quarter have been revised from the movie *Brown Sugar* (Twentieth Century Fox Film Corporation, 2002), which includes replacing the word and concept of *Hip-Hop* to that of *basketball.*

them. The more babies are exposed to language, the more opportunities they'll have to practice their developing communication skills. This is why it is a good idea for caring adult figures to interact with infants and children regularly, speaking with, and reading to him or her whenever possible, which leads to another key developmental task in the first quarter: attachment.

The relationship and quality between the infant and the caregiver(s) bond or attachment affect the child's cognitive and social development. An affectional bond is an enduring tie to a uniquely viewed partner, whereas an attachment is an emotional bond in which a person's sense of security and safe base is bound up in the relationship.[2] For parents to form a strong bond to the infant and child, it is crucial for learning and repetition of mutually reinforcing and interlocking attachment behaviors rather than just immediate contact at birth.

From the ages of two to six years old, the infant moves from dependent baby to independent child. The child can now move around more easily, can communicate more clearly, and has a sense of him or herself as a separate person with specific qualities and has the beginning cognitive and social skills that allow him or her to interact more fully and successfully with peers. Additionally, the child's cognitive abilities are enhancing, becoming less egocentric and tied to outside appearances of things. Their social skills and personality continue to form based on the quality and quantity of social interactions.

From ages six to eleven-twelve years old, physical development is steady and slow with the onset of puberty bringing increased hormonal changes. Additionally, patterns of relationships established in elementary school may have a greater impact on adolescent and adult life than do cognitive changes during this same time period. Moreover, a child's concept of self is more abstract and focused on internal, enduring qualities rather than tied to appearance.

---

[2] Bee, 1998.

There are various influences that can impact normal development in the *First Quarter*. These include the development of genetic anomalies or inherited disease, less-than-optimal family environment (e.g., neglect, abuse, stress, parental/caretaker depression), and/or influences on the family (e.g., economics, healthcare, social support, sociopolitical history, etc.). For example, as African-American families and marriages move from generation to generation, they develop patterns for responding to life crises and life transitions.[3]

These vertical patterns within African-American families and marriages that are passed from generation to generation include family myths, family legacies, family secrets and inherited family interaction patterns. These patterns help families and marriages respond to predictable transitions related to individual, marital, and family lifecycles. In addition, these patterns help families respond to changes caused by unpredictable events confronting the family. These vertical patterns combine with the social and cultural forces that include bicultural challenges or the pressures involved in living in two cultures at the same time, racial oppression, social economic status and religious values, influencing the worldview and values of African-Americans.[4]

This worldview culture of African-Americans specifically serves as a foundation for my socialization process and its impact on my physical, cognitive and social development. Socialization is the process by which children and adults learn from others that begins during the early days of life. Sometimes this learning can be fun and positive that is based on pleasurable and exciting experiences, positive motivation, loving care, and rewarding opportunities. At other times, social learning can be painful and negative where others use punishment, harsh criticism or anger to try to "teach us a

---

[3] Edward P. Wimberly, *Counseling African-American Marriages and Families* (Louisville, KY: Westminster John Knox Press, 1997), pp. 38-50.

[4] Wimberly, pp. 38-50.

lesson." Finally, socialization can occur naturally when infants and children explore, play and discover the social world around them. Whereas planned socialization is mostly a human phenomenon where people make plans for teaching or training others.

TIME-OUT

Throughout this book, we will call a time-out, or a halt in the play (i.e., reading). These time-outs are called strategically at points for you to begin the reflection process of your own spiritual story. As you think about the first quarter, reflect on the following questions as they relate to your life:

- What cultural worldview serves as a foundation for your socialization in the first quarter?
- What vertical patterns, lifecycles (e.g., individual lifecycles, marriage lifecycles, and family lifecycles) and socialization processes have you experienced in the first quarter?
- How did the social and cultural forces in the first quarter influence your physical, emotional, spiritual and relational pain?

Additionally, during slavery African-American families were broken and separated by selling children, parents, and spouses like animals. The long-term historical effects of this type of brokenness and separation can result in multigenerational trauma, manifesting itself psychologically and emotionally in the form of depression, anxiety or post-traumatic stress in members of the family systems. For me, brokenness and separation continued during my generation and within my family system. Charles Stanley's definition of brokenness is as follows:

> "Brokenness is the condition whereby our will is brought into full submission to his will so that when he speaks, we put up no argument, make no rationalizations, offer no excuses, and register no blame, but instead, instantly obey the leading of the Holy Spirit as he guides us."[5]

Spiritual brokenness knows that without God on this journey, we are nothing and can do nothing. Spiritual brokenness is that desire within us to act independently from God. God deals with our brokenness for the purpose of conforming us to his will and making us effective ministers to others (Eph. 2:8-10). Through the adversity, God targets the areas of self-will in our lives. He wants to break the attitudes that do not honor him.

Brokenness is not only a condition it is also a very predictable, planned process from God. It has been said, "When we are the ones being broken it is chaotic and confusing, it is painful and puzzling." Additionally, the only thing that we determine in the process of brokenness is how long we will postpone the inevitable, how long it will take to finally surrender to God's will, shaping us into a servant that resembles His son for maturity and ministry.

Time-Out

- What has been your experience(s) of being socialized into broken and separated families?
- How would you describe your process of spiritual brokenness as a child dependent on the adults in in your life?
- How would you describe your life's journey/process of spiritual brokenness?

---

[5] Charles Stanley.

Theories of Identity Development

Erik Erikson's Stages of Psychosocial Development

Erikson's Developmental Stages is a psychosocial theory that is useful for understanding identity development and self-image across the lifespan. Psychosocial theories refer to the developmental tasks or issues and life events that occur coupled with the person's responses to the issues and adaptations to the events.[6] Erikson thought that identity development resulted from the interaction between inner instincts and outer cultural and social demands. Erikson's theory of development is the most widely recognized theoretical framework for conceptualizing identity across the lifespan.[7]

Within Erikson's theory, the individual must move through and successfully resolve eight "crises" or "dilemmas" over the course of their lifetime to develop a sense of ever-changing self and identity. Each dilemma emerges as the child or adult is challenged by new relationships, new tasks, or new demands. Each dilemma, or stage, is defined by a pair of opposing possibilities with a healthy resolution of each dilemma resulting in the development of a particular strength. However, a "healthy resolution" of each dilemma does not mean moving completely to the apparently positive end of any of the continuum.[8] Healthy development requires a favorable ratio of positive to negative.

A key idea to remember with Erikson's Theory of Psychosocial Development is that each new task, each dilemma, is thrust upon the developing person because of changes in social demands. Whether one likes it or not, age marches along without our permis-

---

[6] Hinkle, 1994.

[7] Allison & Schultz, 2001.

[8] Erikson (1959).

sion and the developing person is confronted with new tasks whether or not she or he has successfully resolved earlier dilemmas. Thus, a person could still be developmentally at the age of 20 while chronologically at the age of 50. You are instead pushed forward, carrying the unresolved issues with you as excess baggage. The very earliest tasks within the *First Quarter* are thus especially important because they set the stage, the journey for everything that follows.[9] It should be noted, however, that each unresolved stage can be resolved successfully at a later time in life.

- **Basic Trust vs. Mistrust**. From ages birth to one year, children begin to learn the ability to trust others based upon the consistency of their caregiver(s). For a successful resolution of this very important foundational task, the caregiver must be consistently loving and have predictable response the child can rely upon. If trust develops successfully, the child gains confidence and security in the world around him or her and is able to feel secure even when threatened. Those children whose early care has been erratic or harsh may develop mistrust, which can result in a sense of fear about the inconsistent world. It may result in anxiety, heightened insecurities, and an over-feeling of mistrust in the world around them. In either case, the child carriers the successful or unsuccessful aspect of basic identity through development, affecting the resolution of later tasks.[10,11]

- **Autonomy vs. Shame, Doubt**. Between the ages of one and three, children begin to assert their independence, by walking away from their primary caretaker, picking which toy to play with, and making choices about what

---

[9] Bee, 1998.
[10] Bee, 1998.
[11] Heffner, 2017.

they would like to wear, to eat, etc. If children in this stage are encouraged and supported in their increased independence, they become more confident and secure in their own ability to survive the world.[12] If children are criticized, overly controlled, or not given the opportunity to assert themselves, they begin to feel inadequate in their ability to survive, and may then become overdependent upon others, lack self-esteem, and feel a sense of shame or doubt in their own abilities.[13] Again, how a child successfully or unsuccessfully resolves this identity development task may also affect the resolution of later tasks.

- **Initiative vs. Guilt**. Around age three or four and continuing to age six, children assert themselves more frequently, begin to plan activities, engage in make-believe play, and initiate activities with others. If given this opportunity, children develop a sense of initiative, and feel secure in their ability to lead others and make decisions. On the other hand, if children's initiative is squelched, either through criticism or control, children develop a sense of guilt. They may feel like a nuisance to others and will therefore remain followers, lacking self-initiative. If unsuccessfully resolved, these behaviors could continue in later childhood, adolescence and adulthood as well as affect the resolution of later developmental tasks.

- **Industry vs. Inferiority**. From age six years to twelve or thirteen, children begin to develop a sense of pride in their accomplishments. They initiate projects, see them through to completion, and feel good about what they have achieved.[14] During this time, teachers,

---

[12] Heffner, 2017.

[13] Heffner, 2017.

[14] Heffner, 2017.

coaches, mentors, pastors, or other important adult figures play an increased role in the child's development. If children are encouraged and reinforced for their initiative socially, academically, and cognitively, they begin to feel industrious and feel confident in their ability to achieve goals. If this initiative is not encouraged, if it is restricted by caretakers, teachers, coaches, mentors, pastors or other important adult figures, the child begins to feel inferior, doubting their own abilities and therefore may not reach their full potential.

How many of you reading this book may not have successfully resolved this task? How many of you as adults still feel inferior, doubting your own abilities? As stated previously, the very earliest tasks within the *First Quarter* are especially important because they set the stage, the journey for everything that follows.[15] If any of these tasks within the *First Quarter* are unresolved, they still can be resolved successfully at a later time in adolescence and/or adulthood.

God will utilize a variety of "tools" throughout your life to break you: (a) by not resolving or achieving developmental tasks, and/or (b) by not having caring adult caretakers, teachers, coaches, mentors, pastors, or other important and caring adult figures. These tools in your laboratory of life include, but are not limited to, God's word (the most powerful tool), your family, home(s), physical and emotional health, friends, and mentors, and failures as well as death and sin to name a few.

Time-Out

- What "tools" in the *First Quarter* did God utilize in your life to break you?

---

[15] Bee, 1998.

- What types of adversity in the *First Quarter* has God allowed in your life to break your self-will, your dependence of others and your independence from Him to transform you into a useful vessel for His kingdom?

Piaget's Theory of Cognitive-Development

A central figure in cognitive developmental theory has been Jean Piaget, who focused on the questions "How does thinking develop?" or "How does a child construct a mental model of the world?" According to Piaget, we are all born with a very basic mental structure on which all subsequent learning and knowledge are built upon. However, as children, thinking is extremely different compared to adults, where by the mechanisms and processes by which the infant, and then the child, develops into an individual who can reason and think using hypotheses. According to Piaget, children construct an understanding of the world around them, then experience discrepancies between what they already know and what they discover (or don't discover) in their environment.[16]

Additionally, to Piaget, cognitive development is a progressive reorganization of mental processes as a result of biological maturation and the social environmental experiences. For the purpose of identifying your spiritual story, social environmental experiences could include those of the individual themselves, the home, the community (i.e., school, places of worship, neighborhood, health services, community agencies, etc.), the extended family, friends, social welfare services, media, neighbors, attitudes and ideologies of the culture, sociohistorical and political conditions and events, just to name a few. According to Piaget, he does not think the environment shapes the child or adult, but the child, like the adult, actively seeks to understand their environment. During the process,

---

[16] Piaget.

the child and the adult explore, manipulate, and examine the objects and people in their world.[17]

Piaget proposed a four-stage theory of cognitive development in which the first three stages occur in the *First Quarter* of an individual's life and the last stage occurs in adolescence, or the *Second Quarter*, and throughout adulthood. These stages reflect the increasing sophistication of children's thoughts marked by qualitative differences rather than a gradual increase in number and complexity of behaviors, concepts, ideas, etc.[18] Each child goes through the stages in the same order, and child development is determined by biological maturation and interaction with the environment. Although no stage can be missed out, there are individual differences in the rate at which children progress through the stages, and some individuals may never attain the later stages. Each stage grows out of the one that precedes it, and each involves a major restructuring of the child's way of thinking. The stages of the first quarter are as follows:

- Sensorimotor (Birth – 18 months/2 years)
    - *Key features*: Focused on only the immediate present, responding to whatever stimuli are available; explores the world by looking, listening, reaching and sucking (e.g., bottle/nipple, thumb, fingers, toys); gradually shifts from not remembering events or things to understanding that objects continue to exist even when they are out of sight and becomes able to remember objects, actions, and individuals over time (i.e., object permanence).
- Preoperational Stage (18 months/2 years – 6/7 years)
    - *Key features*: Begins to use symbols, images, words or actions, that stand for something else; pretend play; egocentric, or only looking at things/situations

---

[17] Piaget.

[18] Bee, 1998.

entirely from own perspective or frame of reference; assumes that everyone sees the world as he or she does; focus is on the appearance of change rather than the underlying, unchanging aspect (i.e., the distinction between appearance versus reality).◦

- Concrete Operational (6/7 years – 11/12 years)
    - *Key features*: New set of skills such as reversibility, addition, subtraction, multiplication, division, and serial ordering; can understand the rule that adding makes something more and subtracting makes it less; that objects can belong to more than one category at once and that categories have logical relationships; develops the understanding that something stays the same in quantity even though its appearance changes; the development of inductive logic, going from the particular to the general, from experience to broad rules; and can work things out internally in their head, rather than physically trying things out in the real world.

The fourth stage, Formal Operational, begins in adolescence at 11/12 years and lasts into adulthood and will be further discussed on the *Second Quarter*. "Piaget thought that virtually all children would move to at least preoperational thought, that the vast majority would achieve concrete operations, but that not all would necessarily achieve formal operations in adolescence or even adulthood."[19]

As a child, not yet able to fully understand the world around you, not able to yet think abstractly, hypothetically deductively and logically, God also utilizes his most powerful tool of his Word to break you. God places various people in your life to prophesize and intercede on his behalf until you are able to mature faithfully and

---

[19] Bee.

spiritually, and discern God's call as well as to acknowledge, be obedient to God, and accept God's call to engage in ministry, whether within the four walls of the physical church or outside.

TIME-OUT

- As you reflect on Erikson's Stages of Psychosocial Development and Piaget's Stages of Cognitive Development, what stages have you been through? What stages do you think you negotiated most successfully? Least successfully? Remember, "Everyone carries some 'baggage' from unresolved issues in earlier life."[20]
- As you reflect over your childhood or *First Quarter* of your life, what signs of God's footprints in your life do you recognize?
- What do you recognize as the role of God in your life within the *First Quarter*, and his interaction that aids to provide significant meaning in your life today as well as a clearer understanding of God's intention for your life?

First Quarter Points of Crisis and God's Presence

Journaling, the writing out of your prayers and God's answers, brings great freedom in hearing God's voice."[21] This is where you will now begin to journal and write your autobiography utilizing questions from the above *Time-Outs* as well as guiding questions from the *Playbook*. "Journaling is a way to hear the Holy Spirit." Habakkuk 2:1-3 states:

---

[20] Beckett & Taylor, 2010.

[21] Andrew Park, *The Holy Spirit DMin Intensive Presentation* (January 28, 2014), accessed March 19, 2014, http://online.united.edu/.

I will stand at my watch and station myself on the ramparts; I will look to see what he will say to me, and what answer I am to give to this complaint. Then the Lord replied: "Write down the revelation and make it plain on tablets so that a herald may run with it. For the revelation awaits an appointed time; it speaks of the end and will not prove false. Though it linger, wait for it; it will certainly come and will not delay."

First, I will share my first quarter spiritual journey.

MY SPIRITUAL STORY

First Quarter

To assist you with beginning the process of journaling and identifying your spiritual story, I will share a brief example of my spiritual story that I identified in my *First Quarter* that forms the foundation for my spiritual autobiography. The story that is recorded and shared in these pages are based on the best of my recollection as well as past and present discussions with friends and family members.

As a child dependent on the adults in my life, my process of brokenness was painful, chaotic, and confusing. I experienced what Erik Erikson defined as identity development crises related to "trust vs. mistrust," "autonomy vs. shame/doubt," "initiative vs. guilt," and "industry vs. inferiority."[22] I experienced grief and loss issues and various traumatic events. God utilized the "tools" in my life including my family, my homes (yes, plural), my physical and emotional health, my friends and my failures as well as death and sin to break me. God began the process of using my adversity to break my self-will, my dependence on others and my independence from Him to transform me into a useful vessel for His kingdom.

The primary agent of socialization and the first "educator," the family, plays an essential role in the transmission of the fundamen-

---

[22] Chris Beckett and Hilary Taylor, *Human Growth and Development*, 2nd ed. (Thousand Oaks, CA: SAGE Publications Inc., 2010), p. 35.

tal values that encourage and nurture learning in a young child. The starting team members of my family included my mother, my biological father, my maternal grandmother, my maternal grandfather and my stepfather. Coming off the bench for the team included other family members such as my three maternal uncles, my maternal sister and brother, my stepbrother, and my step-cousins. Although I identify some of these family members early on as "step," I utilized the word "step" to differentiate my various family members. I have since dropped the word "step" and see them as blood relatives.

Although the song was not released until September 28, 1972, there is a song that clearly describes my biological father during the years before my birth, at my birth, and for at least fifteen years following my birth. "Papa was a rolling stone. Wherever he laid his hat was his home and when he *died*, all he left us was alone.... And Momma, some bad talk goin' 'round town sayin' that Papa had three outside children and another wife, and that ain't right. Folks say Papa never much on thinking. Spent most of his time chasing women and drinking. Papa was a rolling stone. Wherever he laid his hat was his home and when he *died*, all he left us was alone."[23] These lyrics are from the Temptations' single "Papa Was a Rollin' Stone."

As an all-around, handsome, popular, elite athlete in both basketball and baseball, my birth father, unbeknownst to my mother, was no stranger to attracting other women. My birth father was four years my mother's senior. He had many collegiate scholarship opportunities to play basketball and baseball, as well as an offer to play semi-professional baseball in a small town not too far from my mother. Due to an injury, my birth father never made it to professional baseball and ended up working as an electrician at the local university. Today knowing what I know about retirement from sport

---

[23] Norman Whitfield and Barrett Strong, *Papa Was a Rollin' Stone,* remade as a 12-minute record for The Temptations (Detroit, MI: Hittsville USA, 1972).

and identity foreclosure, I would hypothesize that due to his abuse of alcohol and drugs my birth father struggled to transition to life without sports. Additionally, a family member shared with me that my biological father transferred his competitive skills and became a pool shark. His nickname to this day is "Chicago Joe" due to his ruling the tables throughout Illinois, specifically in Chicago, and Colorado.

As part of utilizing the extended family support systems, I was "shipped" down to Illinois for the summer to spend with my maternal grandparents and my two younger maternal uncles. One uncle was eleven years older than me and the other eight years older. During the time that I was with my maternal grandfather, I was able to spend time with my biological father and paternal grandmother. Around the age of seven or eight, I was told a "family secret" that I had brothers (i.e., hidden members of the family) from my childhood friend through vacation bible school at my grandfather's church. I was not aware that I had two brothers, but my friend was my brother's cousin. I found out as an adult that there was a rule that my two brothers and I were to never be together at our paternal grandmother's house nor were we to be discussed with the other.

My maternal grandfather, whom I loved dearly, L. T. Tinsley, distinctively contributed to my personal and spiritual growth. My grandfather instilled in me at an early age that it is just not enough to go to church or listen to spiritual hymns/gospel music. He emphasized that I could not live life lacking faith, not understanding and knowing God's will, and not learning to serve and minister to others. Instead, during this period of development, my maternal grandfather stressed the importance of being aware of who I am as a person and as a spiritual and Christian being, that included understanding my spiritual beliefs and values.

Although my grandfather's values and beliefs were a part of my socialization as a child, they did not become clear to me until I was well into early adulthood. Until adulthood, I sought refuge in school and on the basketball court. My maternal grandfather stressed the importance of spiritual education and knowledge to include the understanding of scripture, hymns, prayer, worship and fellowship. Furthermore, it was important to my maternal grandfather that I develop into a Christian who was able to teach others, to endure trials, to understand the meaning of church membership, to understand Baptist history, and to develop a ministry.

Another major agent of my socialization was school, the primary transmitter of information and knowledge. School for me was called upon to assume many of the functions of the family that includes providing basic needs, before- and after-school programs, and teaching morals and values. The preschool years stand out as the time period when social skills and personality of children and adults are developed. As a result, part of my personality developed based on my experiences of attending a Montessori school and attending school during the 1970s free school movement. Montessori schools utilize a method of observing and following the interests of children.[24] Montessori schools continually adapt the environment from which children learn to that of what children need to know in order to contribute to society, to the environment, and to become fulfilled persons in their particular time and place.[25]

The 1970s free school movement was a student and parent-initiated effort to build small alternative schools.[26] Students participated equally in the free school governance as well as enjoyed complete control over their curriculum.[27] Furthermore, the free school movement integrated multicultural and multilingual edu-

---

[24] The International Montessori Index, *Montessori* (March 21, 2014), accessed March 23, 2014, http://www.montessori.edu/.

[25] The International Montessori Index.

[26] Ron Miller, *Free Schools, Free People: Education and Democracy After the 1960s* (New York: State of New York Publishers, 2002).

[27] Miller.

cation within its curriculum.[28] The movement's goal was to develop free children who would be independent, courageous, and who would be able to deal with the changing complexities of the modern world.[29]

Attending both a Montessori school and the Free School as part of my socialization combined to serve as protective factors against my team—the dysfunctional family system in which I was a part. Research has shown that the combination of a highly vulnerable child and a poor or unsupportive environment can produce the most negative outcomes. However, as a resilient child I was able to do quite well since I was able to find and take advantage of all the stimulation and opportunities available. Although I was part of what I perceived as a dysfunctional, unsupportive environment, my socialization process within the school environment assisted me with coping and overcoming the negative stressors experienced at home.

As part of my socialization in the schools, my peers and some of my family positively influenced my identity development. My social relationships included peers and family members who were integrated in sports, church groups, the classroom, and through service-oriented organizations. As a high-achieving African-American child, I was often ostracized for "talking white," socializing with racially diverse individuals, and achieving academically. Thankfully peers from my sports teams, my maternal grandfather and a step-cousin specifically played a vital role in my development.

My socialization process within the family could be described as one of my spiritual wilderness experiences where it was at times lonely, dark, painful and hopeless. However, as I continued to reflect on my spiritual journey, there were other instances where I

---

[28] George R. Knight, *Issues & Alternatives in Educational Philosophy* (4th ed.). (Berrien Springs, MI: Andrews University Press, 2008).

[29] Knight.

was able to notice God's footprints in my life. There are two separate experiences where my life could have ended from fire. One summer when I was seven years old, I was "shipped" once again to Illinois, this time spending the summer with my step-aunt and her children. I loved one of my step-cousins dearly and wanted to model my demeanor after her strength, courage, and independence. She and I were playing in a homemade dollhouse in the closet on the second floor. Little did we know the back of the house was engulfed in flames! Another step-cousin came and found us and led us out of the house. That day, I witnessed a house burn to the ground.

On a second occasion when I was nine years old, I was home by myself waiting for my step-dad to arrive. Normally, he was at home when I arrived home from school. While home alone, I began to play with matches while sitting on the bathroom toilet, dropping the lighted match in the toilet. There was one lighted match that missed the toilet and dropped on the rug. The fire spread and I tried to fan it out like I had seen done on television. My actions did nothing but spread the fire throughout the bathroom. I ran downstairs and out the door to a neighbor's house and she called the fire department. Because the fire station was two blocks away, they arrived quickly and saved the main floor and basement of our house. Unfortunately, the complete upstairs level was damaged from the fire.

The context of "fire" in my experiences clearly showed the level of God's intention in my life. The HarperCollins Bible Dictionary defines fire as follows:

> Fire was used in the refining of metals, in various crafts, in the waging of war, and in sending messages. Fire also had specialized uses in worship. Fire is a common symbol of holiness and in some cases of protection (Zechariah 2:5). It represents divine action:

> God is called a consuming fire (Hebrews 12:29; Deuteronomy 4:24). Fire is God's servant (Psalms 104:4; Hebrews 1:7), and God's word is like fire (Jeremiah 23:29). In reference to God's action, fire is often a symbol of destruction associated with divine wrath (Genesis 19:24; Exodus 9:23, etc.). Fire can also signify a purging or purifying function (Psalms 66:12; Isaiah. 43:2). In the NT with regard to the sufferings of Christians: their various trials allow the genuineness of their faith to be tested like gold in a refiner's fire (1 Peter 1:6-7).[30]

It wasn't until I started reflecting on the events in my life for my spiritual autobiography that I recognized that God has continually had his hand in my life. He has always been protecting me, watching over me as well as testing my faith, even during my wilderness experiences. This concept became even more relevant once when I was meeting with a client during a counseling session in which she shared her experiences with fire. As I was listening, I was in awe as I had just talked with my step-cousin and my stepfather about the meaning of fire; I had just emailed my step-cousin the spiritual definition of fire. Although one could surmise this was nothing but a coincidence, I clearly knew that the Holy Spirit has been present in my life protecting me and refining me and was present in my office that evening!

Finally, another source of comfort and form of self-soothing, that after reflection was another indication of God's presence in my life, was my passion for music and water. Both the spiritual concepts of music and water allowed me to stay in balance while broken and being tested in the wilderness. As a toddler, my mother

---

[30] Duane L. Christensen, Fire, in *HarperCollins Bible Dictionary,* ed. Mark Allen Powell (New York: HarperCollins, 2011), p. 288.

took many pictures of me wading in the pools. Additionally, she encouraged and pushed me to participate on the swim team. And as an adult, there is not a time when I don't take a vacation that includes the ocean, beach or pool. It has been said, "Water was the primary cosmic element from which all life emerged. Sweet waters were identified with wisdom, fertility and life ... water also conveys ideas of refreshment and power. God is the fountain of living water (Jeremiah 2:13 (AMP)). Jesus offers living water (eternal life)" (John 4:10-15 (AMP)).

Moreover, music was also a source of comfort and form of self-soothing that assisted with keeping me balanced. Music is a powerful tool for transformation and healing. Throughout my lifespan beginning as an infant, music, specifically spiritual and gospel genres, allowed me to relax when stressed and/or overwhelmed. Even today, whenever I am stressed, upset, lonely or hurt, there is not a time I do not listen to traditional and contemporary gospel music. To know that God was ever present in my life, I would connect to him through gospel music. "Connecting to the Source (i.e., God) means also healing. Healing is making something whole, returning it to its natural harmonious state, in alignment with the source."[31] Thus, although there were many points of crises, chaos and confusion during my *First Quarter*, there were also just as many footprints of God that assisted with providing balance, strengthening my faith, conforming me to his will and shaping me into his servant.

---

[31] Javier Ramon Brito, 2012.

YOUR SPIRITUAL STORY

First Quarter

In addition to the questions listed in the *Time-Outs* and the *Playbook*, the following are questions to reflect on and consider as you begin identifying your spiritual story in the first quarter:

- What cultural worldview serves as a foundation for your socialization in the *First Quarter*?
- What vertical patterns, lifecycles (e.g., individual lifecycles, marriage lifecycles, and family lifecycles) and socialization processes have you experienced in the *First Quarter*?
- How did the social and cultural forces in the *First Quarter* influence your physical, emotional, spiritual and relational pain?
- What has been your experience(s) of being socialized into broken and separated families?
- How would you describe your process of spiritual brokenness as a child dependent on the adults in in your life?
- How would you describe your life's journey/process of spiritual brokenness?
- What "tools" in the first quarter did God utilize in your life to break you?

- What types of adversity in the *First Quarter* has God allowed in your life to break your self-will, your dependence of other and your independence from Him to transform you into a useful vessel for His kingdom.

- As you reflect on Erikson's Stages of Psychosocial Development and Piaget's Stages of Cognitive Development, what stages have you been through? What stages do you think you negotiated most successfully? Least successfully? Remember, "Everyone carries some 'baggage' from unresolved issues in earlier life."[32]

- As you reflect over your childhood or *First Quarter* of your life, what signs of God's footprints in your life do you recognize?

- What do you recognize as the role of God in your life within the *First Quarter*, and his interaction that aids to provide significant meaning in your life today as well as a clearer understanding of God's intention for your life?

_____
_____
_____
_____
_____
_____
_____

[32] Beckett & Taylor, 2010.

"Train up a child in the way he should go [teaching him to seek God's wisdom and will for his abilities and talents], Even when he is old he will not depart from it."

(Proverbs 22:6 (AMP))

SECOND QUARTER

ADOLESCENCE (12-18)

Did you ever think you'd see the day basketball grew up? From pick-up on the playground to competitive play in college.

—*Brown Sugar*

Description of the Second Quarter

Adolescence is defined as a time of transition in which significant changes occur physically, cognitively, and socially. Boys experience major pubertal change and girls experience a height spurt and the beginning of their menstrual cycle. Hormonal changes may also increase parent-child conflict and the rise of aggressive or delinquent behavior. The cognitive shift from concrete to formal operations may be central in changes in self-concept, identity formation, moral reasoning, and changes in peer relationships. Self-esteem drops somewhat at the beginning of adolescence due to the transition from middle to high school (and other possible transitions) then rises and continues to rise for the remainder of adolescence with the formation of one's identity, the development of effective coping strategies, and the access of a social support system. The rates of adolescent depression rise sharply and remains high especially for those who may have entered this period of development with lower self-esteem.[33]

---

[33] Bee, 1998.

It should be noted that delinquency and heightened aggressiveness in adolescence are most often forecasted by early development and behavior problems and by inadequate family control as early as toddlerhood.[34] Additionally, first-time adolescents with poorer quality friendships may display antisocial and/or aggressive behavior. By adolescence, and certainly by adulthood, one's toolbox of coping strategies and behaviors are already established.

Multicultural, culture and diversity are not new forces, are ubiquitous, central to each of our lives, and shapes the way we see the world.[35] Although the terms are often used interchangeably, multiculturalism, culture and diversity recognize the broad scope of dimensions of race, ethnicity, language, sexual orientation, gender, age, disability, class status, education, religious/spiritual orientation and other cultural dimensions.[36] The social construction of a cultural identity in adolescence, that are multiple, simultaneous, and ever-shifting, and refers to a person's sense of themselves and their view of themselves, can present particular challenges for individuals across the life span and specifically for young people.[37,38]

Adolescence is the most challenging developmental period with many demands and expectations prior to adulthood. Trying to develop an integrated identity adds to the challenges due to the competing, complex, and very different models of adult identity. Not acknowledging the meaning of some aspect of culture for an individual or not acknowledging the *–ism, -ist*, oppressive and discriminatory attitudes and behaviors in society can restrict the development of a healthy and integrated self with multiple aspects of cultural identity. The lack of clarity about a core identity construct

---

[34] Bee, 1998.

[35] Robinson-Wood, 2017.

[36] Robinson-Wood, 2017.

[37] Beckett & Taylor, 2010.

[38] Robinson-Wood, 2017.

can adversely affect an individual's self-concept, self-esteem, and physical health, and has implications for mental illness symptoms such as depression, anxiety, and post-traumatic stress disorders.

TIME-OUT

- What cultural worldview serves as a foundation for your socialization in the *Second Quarter*?
- What vertical patterns, lifecycles (e.g., individual lifecycles, marriage lifecycles, and family lifecycles) and socialization processes have you experienced in the *Second Quarter*? (For this question, you may have to refer back to the description of the *First Quarter*.)
- How did the social and cultural forces in the *Second Quarter* influence your physical, emotional, spiritual and relational pain?

Theories of Identity Development

- **Erik Erikson's Stage of Identity vs. Role Confusion.** As individuals move from middle childhood to adolescence, the focus shifts from developing industry to developing a personal identity. Adolescence is a time of transition and a time for consolidation where the processes of self-analysis and self-evaluation occur in support of establishing a cohesive sense of self or identity.[39, 40] During this most important and influential stage of identity development, adolescents, in order to resolve this developmental task, must reex-

---

[39] Erikson,1959.
[40] Stryer et al., 1998.

amine their identity in terms of self, career, relationships, families, etc. During this period, they explore possibilities and begin to form their own identity based upon the outcome of their explorations; that is, they are clarifying who they are as individuals and how they relate to others. Adolescents must achieve a reintegrated sense of self, of what he or she wants to do and be, and of their appropriate roles. Because adolescence is the busiest time within the human development lifespan, the risk is that of role confusion arising from the profusion of roles opening up to the adolescent. The sense of who they are can be hindered, which results in a sense of confusion about themselves and their role in the world (i.e., I don't know what I want to be when I grow up).

- **James Marcia's Four Identity Statuses**. Identity statuses are rooted in Erikson's framework of adolescence identity development and consist of a crisis and a commitment.[41] A crisis occurs when adolescents make decisions that question or evaluate past values and choices. A commitment is the outcome of the reevaluation of some specific role or ideology. A crisis and a commitment together create four identity statuses: (a) identity achievement, (b) moratorium, (c) foreclosure, and (d) identity diffusion.[42]

As stated in the *First Quarter,* God utilizes a variety of "tools" throughout your life to break you (a) by not resolving developmental task and/or (b) by not having caring adult caretakers, teachers, coaches, mentors, pastors or other figures in your life. These tools in your laboratory of life include, but not limited to, God's word (the most powerful tool), your family, home(s), physical and emotional

---

[41] Marcia, 1966.

[42] Marcia, 1966.

health, friends, and mentors, and failures as well as death and sin to name a few.

TIME-OUT

- What "tools" in the *Second Quarter* did God utilize in your life to break you?
- What types of adversity in the *Second Quarter* have God allowed in your life to break your self-will, your dependence of other and your independence from Him to transform you into a useful vessel for His kingdom?

Piaget's Stage of Cognitive Development

As also discussed in the *First Quarter*, Piaget proposed a four-stage theory of cognitive development in which the first three stages occur in the *First Quarter* of an individual's life and the last stage occurs in adolescence, or the *Second Quarter*, and throughout adulthood:

- Sensorimotor (Birth – 18 months/2 years)
- Preoperational Stage (2 – 6/7 years)
- Concrete Operational (6/7 – about 11/12)
- Formal Operational (11/12 years – adulthood)

It is important to note that these stages reflect the increasing sophistication of children's thought marked by qualitative differences rather than a gradual increase in number and complexity of behaviors, concepts, and ideas.[43] Additionally, the approximate ages within each stage are a rough guide (i.e., chronological age is not a

[43] Bee, 1998.

criterion).[44] Each child goes through the stages in the same order, and child development is determined by biological maturation and interaction with the social environment. "Although no stage can be missed out, there are individual differences in the rate at which children progress through the stages, and some individuals may never attain the later stages. Each stage grows out of the one that precedes it and each involves a major restructuring of the child's way of thinking." Furthermore, "Piaget thought that virtually all children would move to at least preoperational thought, that the vast majority would achieve concrete operations, but that not all would necessarily achieve formal operations in adolescence or even adulthood."[45]

Key features:
- Possesses the ability to extend concrete operational reasoning abilities to objects and situations that have not been seen or experienced firsthand or that cannot be seen or manipulated directly.
- Instead of thinking only about real things and actual occurrences can now begin thinking about options and possibilities (e.g., thinking about the future systematically). Can imagine future consequences of today's actions so that long-term planning becomes possible.
- Possesses the ability to search systematically and methodically for the answer to a problem.
- Possesses the skill of deductive thinking and logic (e.g., if-then relationships: "If all people are equal, then you and I must be equal."). Can think through a theory to hypotheses.

---

[44] Beckett & Taylor, 2010.
[45] Bee, 1998.

As an adolescent, significant changes occur physically, socially and cognitively. You are facing puberty as well as a whole new set of demands and skills to be learned, new social skills, new and more complex academic and school responsibilities, and identity development. During this time of transition, God also utilizes his most powerful tool of his Word to break you from the same behaviors that are in common with toddlerhood (i.e., negativism, push for independence, egocentrism, and conflict with parents and other adult figures). God places various people in your life to prophesize and intercede on his behalf until you are able to mature faithfully and spiritually, and discern God's call as well as to acknowledge, be obedient to God, and accept God's call to fulfill the plans He has for you, plans for peace and wellbeing, a future and a hope (Jeremiah 29:11 (AMP)).

TIME-OUT

- As you reflect on Erikson's Stages of Psychosocial Development and Piaget's Stages of Cognitive Development, what stages have you been through? What stages do you think you negotiated most successfully? Least successfully? Remember, "Everyone carries some 'baggage' from unresolved issues in earlier life."[46]

- As you reflect over your adolescence or *Second Quarter* of your life, what signs of God's footprints in your life do you recognize?

- What do you recognize as the role of God in your life within the *Second Quarter*, and his interaction that aids to provide significant meaning in your life today as well as a clearer understanding of God's intention for your life?

---

[46] Beckett & Taylor, 2010.

MY SPIRITUAL STORY

Second Quarter

By writing my complaints, hopes and wishes in my journal, I was actually no different than what the Lord stated for Habakkuk do (2:1-3). Habakkuk wrote his complaints to God questioning him on how he could allow an oppressor to continue devouring the righteous. I too questioned God, asking, "Why would you allow certain negative and harsh circumstances to be a part of my life experiences? That includes experiences with my immediate family." I too was looking for God to punish the "oppressor"! So, until then, I had to either sit and wait on God or take matters into my own hands. Initially, I chose the latter.

During the second quarter, I continued my role as I viewed it, as the parentified child. Although my parents had not fully relinquished their parental responsibilities, it was my responsibility to "help" my mother with getting my siblings to daycare and school, prior to me departing for school. Furthermore, it was my responsibility to pick them up from daycare, cook dinner and get them ready for bed. These responsibilities had to be balanced with me completing my schoolwork, working part-time (i.e., delivering newspapers) and playing basketball. I looked forward to the opportunities on the weekend when my mother was home so that I could leave the house to babysit other people's children and/or play pick-up or league basketball.

During middle and high school, my focus was on my academics and on honing my basketball skills. I knew that I would need to attend a college or university as the only way to get away from my immediate context. Additionally, I knew that the only way I was going to attend a college or university was either from obtaining an academic or an athletic scholarship. I became a "wannabe perfectionist" in both areas, as I did not want to let anything get in the way of me being able to leave home.

During seventh grade, I began to incorporate my Christian values and beliefs as well as my knowledge of Christianity within my academic endeavors. My grandfather, L. T. Tinsley, had provided me with pamphlets, which I still have to this day, on the meaning of Baptist Church membership and the Baptist history. I remember how proud he was when I chose to incorporate the Baptist history and the meaning of the Black Church within my English assignment on the book *To Kill a Mockingbird*. Little did I realize then that my spiritual gift of evangelism was beginning to surface.

Moreover, during seventh grade I participated in other sports, including cross-country, track, and swimming in addition to playing basketball. "Many of the developmental problems student-athletes experience result from their attempts to balance conflicting roles, values, and expectations,"[47] that was evident in my case. I was the only African-American on predominantly white teams and it was through these sports that I was able to learn to work with a diverse group of people. Playing sports strengthened my confidence and self-esteem, and I learned to balance sports with other major life activities (i.e., school, family, social). However, while playing basketball in high school, I encountered challenging experiences socially and with my high school basketball coach.

---

[47] Goldberg & Chandler, 1995, p. 39.

During adolescence, student-athletes and non-athletes face a new and complex set of alternative roles and values.[48] According to Erikson's Psychosocial Stages of Development and Marcia's Stages of Identity Development, adolescents unable to integrate new roles and values into a stable personal identity are likely to experience identity confusion or identity foreclosure which is often brought on by the demands of the environment.[49,50] Identity foreclosure may present special challenges for student athletes because their identities may be so "intertwined" with their sport.[51] The challenge arises when a single role becomes dominant. Identity foreclosure "may also be the result of the individual's choosing to forgo engaging in exploratory behaviors and instead opting to commit to the activity in which he or she has previously been rewarded."[52]

An example of being challenged by identity foreclosure in my case would be when I was rewarded for my athletic success and chose not to commit to seeking other academic or personal successes. My focus was to hone my basketball skills so that I could attend college, allowing me to leave home. I invested all of my time and focus in basketball, which impeded me seeking a personal identity beyond that of basketball. Individuals, including me, are likely to detach themselves from other roles and developmental tasks or reduce their motivation to explore alternative roles that again impacted me more in the third quarter.

For me, identify foreclosure occurred when I committed to basketball prematurely without exploring my other needs and values. The consequence of my lack of exploration resulted in frustration and strain in my roles/identity outside of basketball as

---

[48] Stryer et al., 1998.
[49] Erikson.
[50] Marcia.
[51] Stryer et al., 1998.
[52] Danish et al., 1993, p. 355.

well as the lack of search for meaning and understanding of who I was as a person (i.e., role conflict) that impacted me more in the third quarter.

My high school basketball coach, Jerry Miller, and I had what I would describe as a love/hate relationship. We could have been described as oil and water in our interactions. My high school coach always wanted to talk about philosophy, history, the Church and Jesus. All I wanted to do was play basketball. At this time in my life, I did not see or understand the benefit of integrating "church" with basketball. Thus, I gave an attitude to coach. The more attitude I had, the more philosophy, history and bible study we received during practice and following basketball scrimmages and games. All I had to do was *bite the bullet* until I made it to college! I refused to quit the team, as basketball was my ticket to getting out of my immediate situation and going to college. Coach refused to kick me off the team because I was one of his starters my senior year!

Little did I realize that in high school, my basketball coach was actually shaping my identity as a young African-American Christian woman! Additionally, it was through my basketball coach and my team that the role of religion as an agent of socialization continued. Another former student-athlete stated at my high school basketball coach's memorial service:

> "The football field [and basketball court] was his favorite classroom! Here he gave inspirational halftime talks about God and religious homilies about football (and basketball). These boundaries were clear only in Jerry's mind. He made one thing clear to everyone. If Jesus Christ were on earth today, he would be a football [or basketball] player because Jesus Christ was a man of faith and courage. And so was Coach, a man

of faith and courage in life, in the classroom, on the football field and on the basketball court. Faith and courage. A born teacher, he taught us how to live and taught us how to die, with faith and courage."[53]

I appreciate the faith and courage of my high school basketball coach. At a public high school Coach Miller was able to spread the Gospel of Jesus Christ and to assist with my faith walk. My former teammate and my high school basketball coach's daughter, Michelle, shared a letter at his memorial that she received from Coach; the following is a snippet:

> "Teaching and coaching style – first you must establish rapport with the students. When you have them in a group in a teaching situation, don't worry about covering the subject matter.... Talk with them about yourself, your family, your values and your experiences. Show them you are human and share yourself with them first. Later, you sneak into the subject matter.
>
> Second point, as a teacher, coach, parent, you get only get what you demand from them. ... Somehow you must be tough, even if it's basically a bluff.... You must be mean, knowing that it's for the students own good."[54]

What Coach Miller had written clearly helps me to understand his role and responsibility in my life and the development of my identity. And just as Coach Miller always stated, "Truth and God's will are the most important things in life. Jesus meant it when he said,

---

[53] Miller, G. (2012). *Jerry Miller Memorial Part 2 Mr. Hanberg.* Retrieved from https://www.youtube.com/watch?v=onjgcJBJJ6c

[54] Miller, G. (2012). *Jerry Miller Memorial Greg and Michelle Miller.* Retrieved from https://www.youtube.com/watch?v=XZMM1zUc9us

if you do it for the least of these, you do it for me." Although I was not fully aware as an adolescent, I am glad that my Coach Miller was willing and obedient to be used to assist with shaping my identity. Coach Miller will always be a part of me and as an adult I am honored to have had the high school basketball coach that I did, a teacher of basketball and a teacher of life. Most importantly, Coach Miller was a teacher of faith, courage, and action!

My journal writing has been a tool for me to learn how to wait, how to live a life of faithfulness and how to live according to the will of God. The reflection on my life during the *Second Quarter* in the context of how God has been active has revealed patterns and directions that were not evident at the conscious awareness level. Back in 1981-1985, my persistent refusal to hear and heed the Voice of God reduced it to a mere whisper and relegated it to the background of my life. Although I engaged in repeated complaints about my familial injustices and harsh behavior early on in life, today I find my answer in the affirmation "God, the Lord, is my strength," just as Habakkuk responded.

YOUR SPIRITUAL STORY

Second Quarter

In addition to the questions listed in the *Time-Outs* and *Playbook*, the following are questions to reflect on and consider as you begin identifying your spiritual story in the second quarter:

- What cultural worldview serves as a foundation for your socialization in the *Second Quarter*?
- What vertical patterns, lifecycles (e.g., individual lifecycles, marriage lifecycles, and family lifecycles) and socialization processes have you experienced in the *Second Quarter*?
- How did the social and cultural forces in the second quarter influence your physical, emotional, spiritual and relational pain?
- What "tools" in the *Second Quarter* did God utilize in your life to break you?
- What types of adversity in the second quarter has God allowed in your life to break your self-will, your dependence of other and your independence from Him to transform you into a useful vessel for His kingdom?
- As you reflect on Erikson's Stages of Psychosocial Development and Piaget's Stages of Cognitive Development, what stages have you been through? What stages

do you think you negotiated most successfully? Least successfully? Remember, "Everyone carries some 'baggage' from unresolved issues in earlier life" (Beckett & Taylor, 2010).

- As you reflect over your adolescence or second quarter of your life, what signs of God's footprints in your life do you recognize?

- What do you recognize as the role of God in your life within the *Second Quarter,* and his interaction that aids to provide significant meaning in your life today as well as a clearer understanding of God's intention for your life?

_____
_____
_____
_____
_____
_____
_____
_____
_____
_____
_____
_____

"And we know [with great confidence]
that God [who is deeply concerned about us]
causes all things to work together [as a plan]
for good for those who love God,
to those who are called according to
His plan and purpose."

(Romans 8:28 (AMP))

HALFTIME

HALFTIME

In the sport of basketball, halftime is the official suspension of game play between the second and third quarters of a regulation game. During halftime, the two teams exit the court and the coaching staff conducts a meeting in the team's designated locker room. Halftime gives each team time to rest and time to reflect on the first half of the game, making any necessary adjustments based on the way the game has been played. Additionally, during halftime, teams have time to strategize on the best way to win the game during the next two quarters.[55.]

During *Halftime* for this book, this is a time for you meet in your designated locker room or prayer room with God, the Coach. During *Halftime*, rest and reflect on the first half of your life determining what went well and areas that need to be strengthen. Reflect on points of crises of faith in your life, where God's presence was especially vivid and/or challenging, and the outcomes of growth that the crises stimulated (i.e., how the crises affected you). Use this time to strategize and make any necessary adjustments for the second half of your life or to further understand the second half of your life. Continue reflecting on the questions from the *First* and *Second Quarter* as well as from the *Time-Outs* and *Playbook* and write!

[55.] Sporting Charts. (2015). *Sporting Charts explains halftime.* Retrieved from https://www.sportingcharts.com/dictionary/nba/halftime.aspx.

_____
_____
_____
_____
_____
_____
_____

"When I was a child, I talked like a child,
I thought like a child, I reasoned like a child;
when I became a man, I did away with childish things."

(1 Corinthians 13:11 (AMP))

THIRD QUARTER

EARLY ADULTHOOD

(18-30)

The union of basketball to the mainstream was a hard thing to imagine. Basketball was always the personal, regional thing that just belonged to me. Startin' with Magic Johnson and Larry Bird, anyone with a television and a cable box could get a piece of basketball. I knew I was going to have to share and that was a hard thing to get used to.

—Brown Sugar

Description of the Third Quarter

The socialization process during the *Third Quarter* has an enormous impact on children and teens. Family, school, peers, religion, work, volunteer groups, and sports each play a role in the collective process that we call education. Additionally, the socialization process has an enormous impact on one's identity and identity development. In young adulthood, one faces a crisis of developing intimate relationships versus isolation following on from (and building on) the earlier adolescent struggle to establish one's own identity.[56] It is in this quarter that the most important events are love relationships. One is not developmentally complete until they are capable of intimate relationships and share with others. An individual who

---

[56] Beckett & Taylor, 2010.

has not developed a sense of identity usually will fear committed relationships, feel isolated, and unable to depend on anybody in the world as based on Erikson's Stage of Psychosocial Development.[57]

In addition to forming love relationships, Levinson identified four other tasks in early adulthood that include forming and living out a dream, forming mentor relationships, forming an occupation, and forming mutual friendships.[58] Not everyone enters adulthood having successfully resolved developmental tasks from childhood and adolescence that may impact the successful resolution of developing intimate relationships personally, socially, and occupationally. Couple relationships often run into difficulties when one partner wants to continue with the development of their identity and the other does not, which can lead to conflict over whether and when to start a family versus focusing on further education and/or establishing a career.

As the *Third Quarter* is the peak time for physical performance, leaving one's parental home, developing couple relationship, establishing careers, and having children that are culture-specific. Engaging in a couple relationship and/or getting married or leaving one's parents may take place in a very different way.[59] Our sense of who we are and what we do depends on what meaning others make of us and how they convey that meaning back to us, all constructed in the interaction between the individual and others.[60] Additionally, what we do in the *Third Quarter* and our sense of identity is also bound up with our individual and our family history. The interaction between culture and history as well as the successful (or unsuccessful) resolution of early developmental tasks or unfinished business can have powerful effects on individual's processes within the third quarter.

---

[57] Beckett & Taylor, 118.
[58] Beckett & Taylor, 2010.
[59] Beckett & Taylor, 2010.
[60] Campbell, 2000.

TIME-OUT

- What cultural worldview serves as a foundation for your socialization in the third quarter?

- What vertical patterns, lifecycles (e.g., individual lifecycles, marriage lifecycles, and family lifecycles) and socialization processes have you experienced in the third quarter?

- How did the social and cultural forces in the third quarter influence your physical, emotional, spiritual and relational pain?

Erik Erikson's Stage of Psychosocial Development

- **Intimacy vs. Isolation.** This is the first of the three adult stages. The young adult builds upon the identity established in adolescence. During young adulthood, we begin to share ourselves more intimately with others. We explore relationships leading toward longer-term commitments with someone other than a family member. Erikson defines intimacy as "the ability to fuse your identity with someone else's without fear that you're going to lose something or yourself."[61] Successful completion can lead to comfortable relationships and a sense of commitment, safety, and care within a relationship. For those whose identities are weak or unformed, or avoid intimacy, fear commitment and relationships, relationships will remain shallow and the young adult will experience a sense of isolation, loneliness, and sometimes depression.

---

[61] Erikson, 1959.

Chickering's Psychosocial Model of Student Development

- This model of development also serves as a framework for considering the developmental needs of adolescents. Building on the work of Erikson, Chickering described late adolescence and early adulthood as periods when a number of developmental tasks must be accomplished. [62, 63] The seven tasks, or vectors, include developing competence, managing emotions, becoming autonomous, establishing mature relationships, developing purpose, developing integrity, and establishing identity.[64]

Once again, God utilizes a variety of "tools" throughout your life to break you: (a) by not allowing you to resolve, or achieve, a developmental task, and/or (b) by not having caring adult caretakers, teachers, coaches, mentors, pastors, or other caring adult figures. These tools in your laboratory of life include, but not limited to, God's word (the most powerful tool), your family, home(s), physical and emotional health, friends, and mentors, and failures as well as death and sin to name a few.

TIME-OUT

- What "tools" in the *Third Quarter* did God utilize in your life to break you?
- What types of adversity in the third quarter has God allowed in your life to break your self-will, your dependence of other and your independence from Him to transform you into a useful vessel for His kingdom?

---

[62] Valentine & Taub, 1999.
[63] Chickering, 1969.
[64] Valentine & Taub, 1999.

As an adult in early adulthood, you may be taking your place and acquiring, learning, and performing in three major roles central to this stage of development (i.e., worker, spouse/significant other, and parent). However, socially and emotionally, these years are probably more stressful and more difficult than any other part of adulthood.[65] God places various people in your life to prophesize and intercede on his behalf until you are able to mature faithfully and spiritually, and discern God's call as well as to acknowledge, be obedient to God, and accept God's call to engage in ministry.

TIME-OUT

- As you reflect on Erikson's Stages of Psychosocial Development and Chickering's Psychosocial Model of Student Development, what stages do you think you negotiated most successfully? Least successfully? Remember, "Everyone carries some 'baggage' from unresolved issues in earlier life."[66]

- As you reflect over your young adulthood or *Third Quarter* of your life, what signs of God's footprints in your life do you recognize?

- What do you recognize as the role of God in your early adulthood life, or the *Third Quarter*, and his interaction that aids to provide significant meaning in your life today as well as a clearer understanding of God's intention for your life?

---

[65] Bee, 1998.
[66] Beckett & Taylor, 2010.

MY SPIRITUAL STORY

Third Quarter

Prior to graduation from high school, I made the decision to attend Augsburg College, a Lutheran (Evangelical Lutheran Church in America (ELCA)) affiliated Division III institution. I would be introduced to other Christian denominations and the history of religions as part of my academic curriculum. Additionally, I played basketball for four years where I earned multiple athletic accolades and recognitions. My grandfather, L. T. Tinsley, was proud that I was continuing my education at a religiously affiliated college, and knowing this served as a motivator to persevere and graduate despite the relational challenges I endured.

As a parentified child who carried some of the adult responsibility, I carried a sense of entitlement to be taken care of by others because I had lost my childhood. Although I had no choice other than to be a mature and responsible adult, I harbored feelings of anger, resentment, depression and exhaustion that were reflective in my relationships with men. To protect myself and to reduce my anxiety, I tried to avoid the pain, hurt and anger from those unhealed wounds from the first and second quarter through the use of defense mechanisms.

When black men fail to respond to a woman's need of more emotional and verbal expressiveness as well as affection, this often times leads to anger and feelings of rejection and abandonment by black women.[67] Many black women in significant and/or intimate relationships with men feel unappreciated and are deeply angry. The emotional expressiveness demands that I so much sought after could only be met through the quality of the black men in my life being present and empathic, rather than being met by the black men in my life trying to respond by doing some activity to please me.

When I felt anxious and uncomfortable, I found myself early on during the *Third Quarter* utilizing defense mechanisms that impacted my ability to develop intimate relationships. Although there are many types of defense mechanisms, mine mainly came in the form of projection and/or acting out or provoking. Projection is transferring unacceptable thoughts, motives, or impulses to others. Another defense mechanism is acting out with, or provoking, people in our current relationship to respond as others did in our past encounters or relationships. This happened due to my unhealthy and negative coping strategies that were familiar and comfortable.

These defense mechanisms were evident in three specific types of relationships I had early in the *Third Quarter*. The first type of relationship I found myself in mirrored a past relationship with a family member. It represented a harsh, negative, emotional and physically abusive connection. The second type of relationship represented the nice, respectable Christian man in the Church from a well-known respectable, middle-class family that my grandfather wanted. And finally, the last type of relationship represented the "rolling stone." It was with this "rolling stone" that I became pregnant at the age of 23.

Although not the ideal situation to be pregnant without being married, an experience that should be considered a blessing turned out to be a nightmare. The lack of relational and familial support and external stressors combined to result in a miscarriage during the second trimester. Additionally, it was with this "rolling stone"

---

[67] Wimberly, pp. 38-50.

that I almost lost my life due to alcohol and drugs. Thank God for sending a guardian angel (i.e., the nice respectable Christian man) to "save me!"

As I reflect on my past, I realize now that each of the three types of relationship represented the three types of families in which I originated from and was socialized. Wow, what a revelation!

In addition to the challenges I faced with developing intimate relationships, I was challenged with trying to develop a healthy independent and autonomous identity from that of immediate family. During my undergraduate collegiate years, I continued in the role as the parentified parent. I lived on campus but traveled back and forth whenever I was called during a crisis. My being away at college caused our family system to be in disequilibrium. Although I wanted to live my own life, due to the fact that my family role was that of the caretaker/enabler, it was important that during crises I returned home to bring the system back in equilibrium or balance. I learned this from our family and my individual psychologist.

One day out of the blue, I received a phone call from the family psychologist. He asked if I would be willing to meet with him to assist with the understanding of my immediate family dynamics. Of course, I would meet with him! During our first session, he stated, "In every family session, I found that your family was in such disaccord and disequilibrium and that their level of functioning centered around you." He is the psychologist who helped me to understand the dynamics of our family and how it resembled the family system of addiction. Because I was older than eighteen, I was not required to attend the family sessions. However, he asked, "Would you would be willing to attend with the understanding it would benefit your family system and benefit your sister?"

During the first, last and only family session that I attended, "the addict" blew up. They did not want to hear the truths from my views and perspectives of the family, and walked out. "The codependent" just sat there silently and cried; "the mascot" started joking and walked out; "the scapegoat" blew up at an individual family member blaming that person for not saving them; and I "the caretaker/enabler," as much as I wanted to walk out, stayed to soothe and care for a family member.

After this incident, my immediate family never met again for family counseling. Nor did anyone ever talk about the session again for many years. Following this family session, at twenty-two years old, I agreed to participate in individual counseling with the family psychologist, which began my process and journey towards healing. I was committed to the process for two solid years where I worked to finish unfinished business (i.e., hurts, pains and fears) from the past, I worked to strengthen my identity, and I worked on learning to developing healthy intimate relationships with others, which included men.

During my process of individual counseling, on May 23, 1991, my grandfather passed away. It was at this time that I realized that I had matured into a Christian being. I was able to rely on my knowledge of both Christianity and the meaning of life and death as well as rely on my faith to help me through the grieving and mourning process. It was also at this occasion that I knew it was time to fully convert to Christ through confession and baptism. I was baptized on September 1, 1991.

After two years of meeting with the psychologist, I developed the strength and confidence to live my life for me, not my immediate family members. I received a job opportunity working in athletics at a state school in Minnesota. Prior to my departure, I called a family meeting with my immediate family with the purpose of reconciliation and reconciling some unfinished business. Though the family meeting did not turn out as I would have like, I learned that day that I could control my responses to outside triggers. That day, I was able to sing, "I'm free, praise the Lord, I'm free. No longer bound. No more chains holding me. Soul is resting and it's just another blessing. Praise the Lord. Hallelujah, I'm free."[68] That day, I was no longer responsible for their level of functioning as a family. I have not lived in Minneapolis, MN, since 1992!

---

[68] Milton Brunson & Thompson Community Choir, *I'm Free* (1988), lyrics accessed March 19, 2014, http://www.allgospellyrics.com/?sec=listing&lyricid=12987.

YOUR SPIRITUAL STORY

Third Quarter

In addition to the questions listed in the *Time-Outs* and *Playbook*, the following are questions to reflect on and consider as you begin identifying your spiritual story for the third quarter:

- What cultural worldview serves as a foundation for your socialization in the *Third Quarter*?
- What vertical patterns, lifecycles (e.g., individual lifecycles, marriage lifecycles, and family lifecycles) and socialization processes have you experienced in the *Third Quarter*?
- How did the social and cultural forces in the *Third Quarter* influence your physical, emotional, spiritual and relational pain?
- What "tools" in the *Third Quarter* did God utilize in your life to break you?
- What types of adversity in the third quarter has God allowed in your life to break your self-will, your dependence of other and your independence from Him to transform you into a useful vessel for His kingdom?
- As you reflect on Erikson's Stages of Psychosocial Development and Chickering's Psychosocial Model of Student Development, what stages do you think you

negotiated most successfully? Least successfully? Remember, "Everyone carries some 'baggage' from unresolved issues in earlier life" (Beckett & Taylor, 2010).

- As you reflect over your young adulthood or third quarter of your life, what signs of God's footprints in your life do you recognize?

- What do you recognize as the role of God in your early adulthood life, or the *Third Quarter*, and his interaction that aids to provide significant meaning in your life today as well as a clearer understanding of God's intention for your life?

"Train up a child in the way he should go
[teaching him to seek God's wisdom and
will for his abilities and talents],
Even when he is old he will not depart from it."
(Proverbs 22:6 (AMP))

FOURTH QUARTER

MIDDLE ADULTHOOD
(30-60)

Just when you think you know everything there is to know about basketball, it finds a way to surprise you and remind you why you fell in love in the first place.

So what's the difference between sports and basketball? It's simple! It's like the difference between saying you love somebody and being in love with somebody. "Sports" is just a word.

I don't know why your heart doesn't do what your mind tells it.

—Brown Sugar

Description of the Fourth Quarter

It is during the fourth quarter that you have to be aware of any past issues as well as present issues that may impact the successful resolution of this stage. Beckett and Taylor state the following:

> "Many adults in middle years, as well as younger adults, will have had difficulties in dealing with the challenges of earlier stages, and this may make it

more difficult to deal with the new challenges that they now face. And many, however well they faced previous challenges in their lives, will have extra challenges piled on them which they had not expected, and which will force them to radically revise their expectations. In addition, the two things may come together: new challenges and old issues. Old unresolved issues ('baggage', as some people call it, or 'unfinished business') may be brought to a head in middle adulthood by a new crisis that was unexpected but is nevertheless typical of middle adulthood (e.g., difficulties with adolescent children, the break-up of a marriage or long-term relationships, loss of a valued career, the needs of ageing parents, [and sudden and/or traumatic deaths])."[69]

For families, as well as individuals, how they cope with these challenges will depend on their family history. As discussed in the first quarter, these vertical patterns within families and marriages that are passed on from generation to generation include family myths, family legacies, family secrets, and inherited family interaction patterns. These patterns help families and marriages respond to predictable transitions related to individual, marital, and family lifecycles, as well as those changes caused by unpredictable events confronting the family.

Thus, difficulties such as anxiety, stress and depression are likely to occur when something that is happening now, in the present, triggers painful and unresolved issues from the past that make it difficult to successfully complete the changes necessary to deal with the new event. For example, "If you come from a family with a history of difficulties with parenting, the birth of a child will produce

---

[69] Beckett & Taylor, 2010, pp. 126-127.

heightened anxiety, far above the level of anxiety which this new event would produce in other families, or if you come from a family where sexual abuse occurred, there are likely to be anxieties through the generations about physical contact and sex, even assuming that sexual abuse itself doesn't recur through the generations, which it frequently does."[70]

TIME-OUT

- What cultural worldview serves as a foundation for your socialization in the *Fourth Quarter*?

- What vertical patterns, lifecycles (e.g., individual lifecycles, marriage lifecycles, and family lifecycles) and socialization processes have you experienced in the *fourth quarter*?

- How did the social and cultural forces in the *fourth quarter* influence your physical, emotional, spiritual and relational pain?

Erik Erikson's Stage of Psychosocial Development

- Erik Erikson framed middle adulthood generativity vs. stagnation. During this stage of development, the focus is on the adult's ability to look outside oneself, establishing and guiding the next generation, establishing our careers, settling down within a relationship, and to care for others that may include children.[71] Additionally, adults develop a sense of being a part of the bigger picture and give back to society through community activities and organizations. Erikson suggests that adults

---

[70] Beckett & Taylor, 2010, p. 136.
[71] Beckett & Taylor, pp. 119-120.

need children as much as children need adults and that this stage reflects the need to create a living legacy.[72] The positive outcome of this stage is that adults nurture children or help the next generation in other ways. However, there are individuals who, through misfortune or through special and genuine gifts in other directions, do not apply this drive to their own offspring.[73] The negative outcome of this crisis is that an adult could remain self-centered, self-absorbed, and experience stagnation later in life, historically referred to "midlife crisis."

Once again, God utilizes a variety of "tools" throughout your life to break you by not resolving developmental task, by not having caring adult caretakers, teachers, coaches, mentors, pastors or other caring adult figures. These tools in your laboratory of life include, but are not limited to, God's word (the most powerful tool), your family, home(s), physical and emotional health, friends, and mentors, and failures as well as death and sin to name a few.

TIME-OUT

- What "tools" in the *Fourth Quarter* did God utilize in your life to break you?
- What types of adversity in the *Fourth Quarter* has God allowed in your life to break your self-will, your dependence of other and your independence from Him to transform you into a useful vessel for His kingdom?

In middle adulthood, three particular events are significant that in-

---

[72] Beckett & Taylor, pp. 119-120.
[73] Beckett & Taylor, pp. 119-120.

cludes one's health, the timing of family and work events, and the existence of crises and unanticipated life changes. Again, God utilizes his most powerful tool of his Word to break you. God places various people in your life to prophesize and intercede on his behalf until you are able to mature faithfully and spiritually, and discern God's call as well as to acknowledge, be obedient to God, and accept God's call to engage, or further engage, in ministry in ministry.

TIME-OUT

- As you reflect on Erikson's Stages of Psychosocial Development, what stage do you think you negotiated most successfully? Least successfully? Remember, "Everyone carries some 'baggage' from unresolved issues in earlier life."[74]

- As you reflect over your middle adulthood or *Fourth Quarter* of your life, what signs of God's footprints in your life do you recognize?

- What do you recognize as the role of God in your life within middle adulthood, or the *Fourth Quarter*, and his interaction that aids to provide significant meaning in your life today as well as a clearer understanding of God's intention for your life?

---

[74] Beckett & Taylor, 2010.

MY SPIRITUAL STORY

Fourth Quarter

The time period in my life that has been influential to my personal, Christian and spiritual growth was from 1997-2014. While an undergraduate student at Augsburg College, the director of the Black Student Union, M. Anita Gay-Hawthorne, served as my mentor, spiritual advisor, and "mom." It was through Anita's guidance that I developed an identity outside of basketball, gained confidence as a young African-American woman, and clarified my career goals. Anita was one of those people who I felt God placed in my life for a reason and was a necessary component to my personal, Christian and spiritual growth.

On November 21, 1997, I visited Augsburg College to surprise Anita. I had been offered an athletic advising position at the University of Pittsburgh, and as I had in the past, I wanted to talk with her about my options. While we were meeting she shared how proud she was of me. She encouraged me to take the job. "Pittsburgh is where you belong!" Little did I know that this would be the last time that I would see and talk to M. Anita Gay Hawthorne. Anita passed away in January 1998, one week after I moved to Pittsburgh. I know today that it was in God's will for me to see Anita in November 1997 and for me to move to Pittsburgh. I truly feel Anita allowed God to use her to speak to me. Again, this awareness and knowledge was so very influential in my personal, Christian and spiritual growth.

Because I had just started my job in Pittsburgh, I was unable to go home to Minneapolis, MN, for Anita's funeral. It was my plan to sit in the sanctuary at one of the churches that I was considering for my new church home in Pittsburgh, PA, concurrent to Anita's funeral. I chose a church that resembled both my maternal grandfather's church (also my paternal grandmother's church) and my maternal grandmother's church. My grandparents went to two different churches, one more traditional and the other more contemporary. While visiting Mount Ararat Baptist Church (MABC) during the time of Anita's funeral, a couple ministers came in the sanctuary *with* me and prayed. It was at this time that I knew MABC was my new church home! When God closes one door, he opens another. I became an official member of MABC on July 5, 1998.

As a family member at MABC, I continued to grow and mature in terms of my personal Christian and spiritual awareness and knowledge. Additionally, I was able to utilize my spiritual gifts, skills and techniques within the youth ministry and the usher board. I was nourished through prayer, worship, bible study, fellowship and involvement. However, in 2001 and 2002, my faith in God was once again tested. I lost both my 25-year-old step-cousin, who died giving birth, and my 24-year-old maternal brother, who was killed by a stray bullet. Both died due to sudden and traumatic experiences. I just could not understand why God would have allowed me to experience so many significant deaths so close together.

Although I was angry and depressed, I realized that I was spiritually mature enough not to lose my faith completely. I remember in 2002, my daily scripture reading was Matthew 17:20 (NIV): "He replied, "Because you have so little faith. I tell you the truth, if you have faith as small as a mustard seed, you can say to this mountain, move from here to there' and it will move. Nothing will be impossible for you." This scripture became the impetus for the next stage of my life's journey.

While grieving and mourning the death of my brother, a good friend came to me, stating, "You need to get your act together." She further stated, "Your brother would not want you lying around depressed. He would want you to get up and begin helping others who may need support dealing with loss, death and grief." It was through my friend's influence and spiritual guidance that I found Duquesne University in Pittsburgh, PA. Duquesne University is an institution built on Catholic-Spiratan traditions and it is where I received my Ph.D. in Counselor Education and Supervision. Moreover, Duquesne University is where I further grew as a spiritual being. My Christian and spiritual growth further matured and my skills utilizing Christian and spiritual interventions within the counseling process was strengthened.

While completing my requirements at Duquesne University in 2005, I was simultaneously dating. Once again, I found myself pregnant ... with twins! Although it was not my plan or intention to pursue a lifelong intimate relationship with this person, we did agree that we could and would work together to raise the children. The day before my graduation from Duquesne University, I had yet another miscarriage. My faith was tested once again. Again, I encountered internal tension between being happy and celebrating the awarding of my degree and grieving and mourning the loss of my twins in their second trimester.

This internal tension continued on March 8, 2008, when my maternal uncle, eleven years my senior, passed away. We had been socialized together as children, and as I mentioned before, he took on the role of a big brother. My uncle had a way of taking care of me and protecting me, especially during my middle school and high school years when he moved to Minneapolis, MN. I often wonder if my grandfather had something to do with my uncle moving to Minnesota to watch over my family. Although I was no longer "shipped" to Illinois, after I shared with my grandfather what was happening in my immediate household, my uncle appeared! God sure does send individuals into one's life to prophesize, to intercede on his behalf, and to watch over and protect. He has done this in my life until I have been able to mature faithfully and spiritually, and discern God's call to engage in his ministry.

To further the tension that I was feeling from mourning the loss of my uncle, I was also dealing with the rejection and avoidance of a particular family member. I balanced the tension with excitement of finally being able to have an open relationship with the paternal side of the family, including my paternal siblings. I was excited to be reunited with my paternal brother, four months my senior. Although we did not inform our families, when we were eighteen years old, my two paternal brothers and I reached out to each other to begin developing a relationship. However, at my maternal uncle's funeral, my older paternal brother decided to attend the repast. This was the first time in forty-one years that we chose to be in the same room with each other in Champaign, IL, around family and friends. Although we both experienced some anxiety, together we were able to exert our strength and support one another.

One particular family member was not happy and clearly let me know, "Having him around causes too much pain. It would be best if you did not bring him around us." I was so taken aback, not understanding how I could not be supported in the reunification of my siblings. I did not understand, considering that it was not a problem, that it was okay that some of my immediate and extended family included siblings with different fathers unified with their mothers.

I have had glimpses of God's handiwork as it relates to the restoration and unification of my family. As I reflect on my family brokenness, I do realize that restoration of the family will happen in God's time, when we humble ourselves by forgiving and praying for one another. Although I have experienced a wealth of emotional, spiritual and relational pain from my family's brokenness, I know that without God on this journey, I am nothing and can do nothing, just as it was with Abraham and with Joseph's family in the book of Genesis.

In my Christian tradition and community, "the staple of our religion and the foundation of our spirituality is faith."[75] The practical step that I would need to grow in faith in my community is to understand that there are others in history that fought the battle of faith and were commended for their faith. I need to understand spiritual development and exactly what faith is. It is my hope that I can continue on my faith journey to be faithful and disciplined enough as both Abraham and Joseph were. And, as I continue to strengthen my relationship with God, I know that I will continue to be called and tested. However, history does matter in that God has provided evidence that he has fulfilled his commandment in the past and will continue to do so today and tomorrow!

---

[75] William H. Curtis, *Faith Learning to Live Without Fear, A Guide to Faith and Overcoming Challenges* (Pittsburgh, PA: William H. Curtis Ministries, 2010), p. 24.

YOUR SPIRITUAL STORY

Fourth Quarter

In additions to the questions listed in the *Time-Outs* and *Playbook*, the following are questions to reflect on and consider as you begin identifying your spiritual story in the *Fourth Quarter*.

- What cultural worldview serves as a foundation for your socialization in the *Fourth Quarter*?
- What vertical patterns, lifecycles (e.g., individual lifecycles, marriage lifecycles, and family lifecycles) and socialization processes have you experienced in the *Fourth Quarter*?
- How did the social and cultural forces in the *Fourth Quarter* influence your physical, emotional, spiritual and relational pain?
- What "tools" in the *Fourth Quarter* did God utilize in your life to break you?
- What types of adversity in the *Fourth Quarter* has God allowed in your life to break your self-will, your dependence of other and your independence from Him to transform you into a useful vessel for His kingdom?
- As you reflect on Erikson's Stages of Psychosocial Development, what stage do you think you negotiated most successfully? Least successfully? Remember,

"Everyone carries some 'baggage' from unresolved issues in earlier life" (Beckett & Taylor, 2010).

- As you reflect over your middle adulthood or *Fourth Quarter* of your life, what signs of God's footprints in your life do you recognize?

- What do you recognize as the role of God in your life within middle adulthood, or the *Fourth Quarter*, and his interaction that aids to provide significant meaning in your life today as well as a clearer understanding of God's intention for your life?

"Let no one look down on [you because of] your youth, but be an example and set a pattern for the believers in speech, in conduct, in love, in faith, and in [moral] purity."

(1 Timothy 4:12 (AMP))

OVERTIME

OLDER ADULTHOOD

(60-Death)

I always thought, one day I would outgrow my relationship with basketball. I never thought it was a "fad" like many, but I never thought it could grow and mature. I thought it would be an adolescent memory I'd look back on, like a crush on the captain of the football team. But I realize we have more than that, much more. We have a history, a friendship, we listen to each other, we laugh together, we finish each other's plays. I don't have to pretend with basketball and basketball doesn't have to pretend with me. My feelings have never been more clear and I know they will never go away.

—*Brown Sugar*

Description of Overtime

It is during this time that older adults contemplate their accomplishments and are able to develop integrity if they see themselves as leading a successful life. Older adults need to look back on life and feel a sense of fulfillment. Success at this stage leads to feelings of wisdom, while failure results in regret, bitterness, and despair.[76]

---

[76] Erikson, 1959.

What Is Successful Aging?

- **Biomedical Theory.** "Defines successful aging largely in terms of the optimization of life expectancy while minimizing physical and mental deterioration and disability."[77] The focus is on the absence of chronic disease and of risk factors for disease, good health, and high levels of independent physical functioning performance, mobility and cognitive functioning.

- **Psychosocial Development Theory.** Emphasizes successful aging as life satisfaction, social participation and functioning, and psychological resources, including personal growth. "Satisfaction with one's past and present life has been the most commonly proposed definition of successful aging and includes zest, resolution and fortitude, happiness, relationships between desired and achieved goals, self-concept, morale, mood and overall wellbeing."[78] The definition also encompasses high levels of ability in social role functioning, positive interactions or relationships with others, social integration, and reciprocal participation in society.

- **Lay Views.** Main Constituents of Successful Aging:[79]
    - Life expectancy
    - Life satisfaction and wellbeing (includes happiness and contentment)
    - Mental and psychological health, cognitive function
    - Personal growth, learning new things
    - Physical health and functioning, independent functioning

---

[77] Bowling & Dieppe, 2005, p. 1548.

[78] Bowling & Dieppe, 2005, p. 1549.

[79] Bowling & Dieppe, 2005, p. 1549.

- Psychological characteristics and resources, including perceived autonomy, control, independence, adaptability, coping, self-esteem, positive outlook, goals, sense of self
- Social, community, leisure activities, integration and participation
- Social networks, support, participation, activity
- Enjoyment of diet
- Financial security
- Neighborhood
- Physical appearance
- Productivity and contribution to life
- Sense of humor
- Sense of purpose
- Spirituality

Strategies for Successful Aging

Successful aging is more dependent on behavior, attitude, and environment than on hereditary traits. Current strategies include:[80]

- Exercising****
- Eating healthy and restricting calories intake
- Quitting smoking and substance use
- Obtaining appropriate healthcare
- Seeking help for mental illnesses such as depression****
- Develop cognitive and psychological strategies such as positive attitude, resilience, and reducing stress.

---

[80] Depp, Vahia, & Jeste, 2010.

- Seek and give support through volunteering, working in a group, learning new skills, mentoring younger individuals.

****Very Critical to Successful Aging and Adult Development

The developmental tasks of successful aging in *Overtime* are affected by the perception of the individual, family, community and society as a whole. Specifically, for older adults, ageism, or the discrimination against people because of their age, is a social and cultural factor that needs to be considered. Robinson-Wood states:

> "Unlike most traditional cultures in which the elderly tend to be respected and valued, in the U.S. culture, inordinate emphasis is placed on youthfulness. The society significance attached to doing, productivity, and maintaining mastery over nature may explain this cultural preoccupation with youth and the herculean effort to defy and, in some instance, deny or defeat aging. Aging appears to be viewed as a loss of control and of diminishing power and beauty. Discrimination against a segment of the population that is composing a higher percentage of the total and of which all will be members, if they are fortunate, culminate in fear-based discourses about the experience of being an elder. It is heartening to see how a culture of menopausal women is redefining hot flashes as power surges and recognizing the "change" in life as a time of ascendancy and coming into one's own."[81]

---

[81] Robinson-Wood 2017, p. 53.

TIME-OUT

- What theory of successful aging serves as the foundation for your socialization in *Overtime*?

- What cultural worldview serves as a foundation for your socialization in *Overtime*?

- What vertical patterns, lifecycles (e.g., individual lifecycles, marriage lifecycles, and family lifecycles) and socialization processes have you experienced in *Overtime*?

- How did the social and cultural forces in overtime influence your physical, emotional, spiritual and relational pain?

Erik Erikson's Stage of Psychosocial Development

- Ego Integrity vs. Despair. As we transition into older adulthood and become senior citizens, retirement is in the horizon and productivity may slow down. It is during this time that we contemplate our accomplishments and are able to develop integrity if we see ourselves as leading a successful life. If we see our lives as unproductive, feel guilty about our pasts, or feel that we did not accomplish our life goals, we become dissatisfied with life and develop despair, often leading to depression and hopelessness.[82]

Older adulthood is a time when many large and small roles are shed (e.g., spouse, career), there are changes in the demands of many social roles as well as a decline in health and biological functioning take place, if not used regularly. As an adult, you negotiate between ego integrity or coming to terms with who you are and have been, how your life has been lived, the choices that you have made and

---
[82] Beckett & Taylor.

the opportunities gained in loss and despair or feeling as though your life has been unproductive, feeling guilty about the past, dissatisfied with life, feeling depressed and/or feeling hopeless. God places various people in your life to prophesize and intercede on his behalf until you were able to mature or further mature faithfully and spiritually, and discern God's call as well as to acknowledge, be obedient to God, and accept God's call to engage in ministry.

TIME-OUT

- As you reflect on Erikson's Stages of Psychosocial Development, what aspect of the stage of integrity vs. despair do you think you negotiated most successfully? Least successfully? Again, remember, "Everyone carries some 'baggage' from unresolved issues in earlier life."[83]

- As you reflect over your late adulthood, or the *Overtime* of your life, what signs of God's footprints in your life do you recognize?

- What do you recognize as the role of God in your life during older adulthood or *Overtime*, and his interaction that aids to provide significant meaning in your life today as well as a clearer understanding of God's intention for your life?

---

[83] Beckett & Taylor, 2010.

MY BUDDING SPIRITUAL STORY

Overtime

A spiritual autobiography is not meant to be a comprehensive chronicle of your spiritual journey, but rather a selective reflection on events, periods, influences, people and experiences that you are led to write about. Although there is much more that I could include in my spiritual stories throughout this book, the purpose is to draw the strands of my life together in a way that points me to my meaning and assists you with finding meaning in your own life. Although, Lord willing, I still have to journey through and finish my *Fourth Quarter* and successfully navigate the *Overtime* of my life, at this point I now have a better understanding of the new level of God's intention for my life.

Today, I am more aware and confident with the trials and tribulations of life and that it is those challenging experiences that have contributed to my spiritual growth and total wellness. I realize wholeheartedly that in Christ, living is growing, and growing is living. My life's journey has become more disciplined, full and joyful that has allowed me to utilize my spiritual gifts in my current ministry both inside and outside the mortar brick walls of the physical church.

My grandfather, L. T. Tinsley, instilled Matthew 28:19-20 in me at a young age. This verse provides the foundation of the purpose of my ministry inside and outside the mortar brick walls of the physical church:

> "Go ye therefore, and teach all nations, baptizing them in the name of the Father, and of the Son, and of the Holy Ghost, teaching them to observe all things whatsoever I have commanded you: and, lo, I am with you always, even unto the end of the world. Amen" (Matthew 28:19-20 KJV).

I have served in the Mount Ararat Counseling Center and Transitions Counseling Service, LLC, among other areas in the community. Additionally, I utilize my Christian and spiritual awareness and knowledge as well as my spiritual gifts within my role as a counselor educator, clinical supervisor, and spiritual leader that are also influential factors that contribute to my personal, Christian and spiritual growth on a daily basis.

God has been working in my life to lead me to ministry that is developmental, diverse and multifaceted. My philosophy of the role, importance, and responsibility of the local church stems from my involvement in the Church from a young age to the present day, and from my knowledge of the role of the history of the black church. I believe that the role of the local church is to help families define the meaning and mission of their existence in a culturally diverse society. The Church should help to educate and empower individuals, groups and families to live amidst adversity and changing family values and patterns. I believe the Church has a responsibility to provide for, and assist, its congregants and the individuals from the community from which the Church is located with preventative programs and interventions that focus on the wellness model (i.e., spiritual, family, career/occupational, physical, emotional, and intellectual development). Additionally, it is the Church's responsibility to advocate for our congregants and for the communities in which we serve on social and political issues that may impact their wellbeing.

> "He has showed you, O man, what is good.
> And what does the LORD require of you?
> To act justly and to love mercy and to walk humbly
> with your God."
>
> (Micah 6:8)

It is also my belief that the calling of the Church today in matters of doing justice and loving mercy is providing a ministry of care and counseling. This ministry of care and counseling, also known as pastoral care, in which all members of the Church should provide, "is focused upon the healing, guiding, supporting, reconciling, nurturing, liberating, and empowering of people in whatever situation they find themselves."[84] We are living in a world that is forever changing, including the culture and diversity of the world. It is important that the Church provide cultural relevant ministry (i.e., self-awareness, worldview knowledge, culturally appropriate skills and interventions while developing cross-cultural relationships, and incorporate the principles of morality (i.e., autonomy, do no harm, beneficence, justice and fidelity).

Both Jesus and Paul in their historical contexts were multicultural competent prophets, ministers, and teachers. As members of the body of Christ, we too must also learn to exegete ourselves and the surrounding culture and cultural context to reach people culturally and developmentally with the gospel message. The Church both inside and outside the mortar brick walls of the physical church must continue to engage in social justice, social change, that reconciles brokenness with God, with self, with others, and with creation back towards peace and harmonious relationships.

---

[84] Bruce Rumbold, *Pastoral Care* (Melbourne Victoria, Australia: La Trobe University School of Public Health, N.D.), accessed June 23, 2019, from http://www.pastoralcareact.org/what-is-pastoral-care/.

YOUR SPIRITUAL STORY

Overtime

In addition to the questions listed in the *Time-Outs* and *Playbook*, the following are questions to reflect on and consider as you begin identifying your overtime spiritual story:

- What theory of successful aging serves as the foundation for your socialization in *Overtime*?
- What cultural worldview serves as a foundation for your socialization in *Overtime*?
- What vertical patterns, lifecycles (e.g., individual lifecycles, marriage lifecycles, and family lifecycles) and socialization processes have you experienced in *Overtime*?
- How did the social and cultural forces in overtime influence your physical, emotional, spiritual and relational pain?
- As you reflect on Erikson's Stages of Psychosocial Development, what aspect of the stage of integrity vs. despair do you think you negotiated most successfully? Least successfully? Again, remember, "Everyone carries some 'baggage' from unresolved issues in earlier life."[85]
- As you reflect over your late adulthood, or the *Overtime*

---
[85] Beckett & Taylor, 2010.

of your life, what signs of God's footprints in your life do you recognize?

- What do you recognize as the role of God in your life during older adulthood or *Overtime*, and his interaction that aids to provide significant meaning in your life today as well as a clearer understanding of God's intention for your life?

_____
_____
_____
_____
_____
_____
_____
_____
_____
_____
_____
_____

"He has made everything beautiful and appropriate
in its time. He has also planted eternity [a sense of
divine purpose] in the human heart [a mysterious longing
which nothing under the sun can satisfy, expect God]
yet man cannot find out (comprehend, grasp) what God
has done (His overall plan) from the beginning to the end.
I know that there is nothing better for them
than to rejoice and to do good as long as they live."
(Ecclesiastes 3:11-12 (AMP))

POST-GAME

POST-GAME

The purpose of this book was to introduce you to the importance of understanding your spiritual story and the development of a spiritual autobiography of your personal and professional development. When you reflect on your life and your spiritual story in the context of the themes presented within each quarter you may reveal patterns and directions that you were not fully aware of before now. This book is designed for you to identify your spiritual story and develop your spiritual autobiography that encourages you to frame your experiences in a new way. You may find yourself coming to a greater appreciation for and trust in the direction of your life, or you may find that you are able to articulate challenges and periods of difficulty in new transformative ways.

Self-understanding is a key to an effective ministry both inside and outside the physical walls of the church building. Your spiritual autobiography should describe who you are as it relates to your current context or your developing ministry, who you are as one who proclaims the Word of God, and where God has sent you to serve. This book is designed to help you better understand whom God has made you to be, how God has used life's circumstances and the people in your life to help shape you. What you learn as a result of identifying your spiritual story and transforming your spiritual autobiography will ultimately help you shape your proposed or current ministry.

Additionally, the purpose of this book is to assist you with identifying and analyzing life experiences from a cultural and development perspective that aids with understanding your career, ministerial or community focus. I am a true believer that God allows you to go through your challenging, and possible painful, life experiences and heals you so that you can go back into those same places to minister, counsel, teach, and help others to heal. Often times, we as human beings avoid certain calls to ministry or specific career fields due to a lack of self-awareness and knowledge of the purposes of our life's journey (Psalm 139:1-18 (CEB). For as the Lord states in Jeremiah 17:10 (NIV), he knows the plans he has for you, plans to prosper you, plans to give you hope and a future. The amplified version of Jeremiah 17:10 states: "For I know the plans and thoughts I have for you, plans for peace and wellbeing and not for disaster to give you a future and a hope." Thus, God wants you to critically evaluate your life's circumstances and the important people in your life that is designed to shape you. As part of our spiritual walk, God wants us to understand that:

- We are spiritual beings encased in physical bodies;
- Before we ever physically walked on the face of the earth, we traversed it with God, in the Spirit; and
- His plan and purpose for us, now, is to walk out our journey in the flesh, guided by His Spirit in order to reach our destiny in the earth.

We are now walking out what God has already planned, a portion of your destiny. The walking out of that journey and the understanding of it is assisted by writing, journaling of our spiritual autobiography.

POST-GAME INTERVIEW

- Because of who you are becoming, how will it impact your ministry or your service in the community (i.e., your approach, your rationale, your theoretical approach, etc.)?
- What ministry, career field, and/or community service opportunity is being developed/shaped in you?
- What drives the urgency in you to become a leader in your specific context? What drives you to be an accomplished leader?
- Write about an experience which gives a sense of what you care deeply about and why.
- Write about a conversation or debate with a friend, or a telling depiction of how your family spends its time, or some moment when you realized that you couldn't believe what others seemed to want you to believe.
- Write about playing basketball or riding horses or making music—whatever you love to do.

Following the post-game debriefing and interview session, the team regroups, views films (i.e., past life experiences), and begins practicing for the next game, the next season or quarter of one's life. Use this time as an opportunity to understand your own spiritual story, share your story in small groups, share with spiritual leaders, share with those you are ministering to, inside and outside of church walls and/or share with your classmates, family and friends. Remember, church is where two or three gather in His name, for there He is with you, whether inside a physical building our outside (Matthew 18:20).

Just as the Lord has examined you (Psalm 139), it's time for you to examine yourself. So now, go write! In other words, write about anything which conjures up for you a sense of how you came to be the person you are still becoming, or what your ultimate values or convictions might be. Enjoy and trust the process!

> "Have I not commanded you?
> Be strong and courageous!
> Do not be terrified or dismayed (intimidated),
> for the Lord your God is
> with you wherever you go."
>
> (Joshua 1:9 (AMP))

PLAYBOOK

Spiritual Autobiography Components

While the spiritual autobiography can contain a plethora of ingredients, there are several key components that should be included. A spiritual autobiography is not meant to be a comprehensive chronicle of one's spiritual journey, but rather a selective reflection on events, periods, influences, people and experiences that you are led to write about. The following are a listing of questions or components, in addition to those listed in each *Quarter, Overtime,* and *Time-Out,* to consider when beginning to identify your spiritual story:

- Who were you? This question deals with your formative years.
- Who impacted you?
- How has it affected you?
- Who are you now? From all that you have endured, who have you become?
- Because of who you are becoming, how will it impact your philosophy and theory of ministry? For this question, you will need to clearly define your ministry perspective whether within or outside the mortar brick walls of the physical church.
- What were your parents' and grandparents' spiritual/religious practices? Religious affiliation?

- What early messages about God did you receive from your family? (i.e., parents, grandparents, etc.).
- What were your earliest experiences/memories about religion? Spirituality? God?
- What were the significant good memories? Significant bad memories?
- How did you celebrate religious holidays?
- What were your earliest impressions about sin? Guilt/shame? Salvation? How have those changed?
- What were your impressions about death/the afterlife? How have those changed?
- What was your conversion experience or experiences? This allows room for multiple turning points.
- Who were the most influential people in your spiritual life?
- Were there any crises or periods of doubt? Describe them and how you resolved them, if you have.
- Were there any books, stories (written and/or oral), scripture passages, etc., that influenced you? Why are those so important to you?
- Who are you now (i.e., spiritually, intellectually, socially, occupationally, etc.)? From all that you have endured, who have you become? What was this process like for you? What patterns do you notice?

BIBLIOGRAPHY

Allison, B. N., & Schultz, J. B. (2001). Interpersonal identity formation during early adolescence. *Adolescence, 36,* 509-523.

Beckett, C., & Taylor, H. (2010). *Human Growth and Development* (2nd ed). Thousand Oaks, CA: SAGE Publications Inc.

Bee, H. (1998). *Lifespan Development* (2nd ed.). New York: Addison-Wesley Educational Publishers, Inc.

Bowling, A., & Dieppe, P. (2005). *What is successful ageing and who should define it?*, *BMJ,* 331 (7531), 1548-1551. doi: 10.1136/bmj.331.7531.1548. Retrieved from https://www.ncbi.nlm.nih.gov/pmc/articles/PMC1322264/

Brito, J. R. (2012). *Heal with music. Discover the secret healing power of spiritual music.* Retrieved from https://www.personal-growth-can-be-fun.com/HealwithMusic.html.

Brunson, Milton & Thompson Community Choir. (1988). *I'm Free.* Retrieved from http://www.allgospellyrics.com/?sec=listing&lyricid=12987

Campbell, D. (2000). *The socially constructed organization.* London: Karnac Books Ltd.

Chickering, A. W. (1969). *Education and Identity.* San Francisco, CA: Jossey-Bass.

Christensen, D. L. (2011). "Fire." In *HarperCollins Bible Dictionary,* edited by Mark Allen Powell. New York: HarperCollins, 288.

Curtis, W. H. (2010). *Faith Learning to Live Without Fear, A Guide to Faith and Overcoming Challenges.* Pittsburgh, PA: William H. Curtis Ministries.

Danish, S. J., Petitpas, A. J., & Hale, B. D. (1993). Life development intervention for athletes: Life skills through sports. *The Counseling Psychologist, 21*, 352-385.

Depp, C., Vahia, I. V., & Jeste, D. (2010). Successful aging: Focus on cognitive and emotional health. *Annual Review of Clinical Psychology, 6*, 527-550.

Erikson, E. H. (1959). Identity and the lifecycle. *Psychological Issues, 1*, 1-171.

Goldberg, A., & Chandler, T. (1995). Sports counseling: Enhancing the development of the high school student athlete. *Journal of Counseling and Development, 74*, 39-44.

Heffner, C. L. (2017). *Erikson's stages of psychosocial development.* Retrieved from http://allpsych.com/psychology101/social_development.html

Hinkle, J. (1994). Integrating sport psychology and sports counseling: Developmental programming, education, and research. *Journal of Sport Behavior, 17,* 52-49.

Hudson, Hugh, (Director). (1981). *Chariots of Fire* [Motion Picture]. Enigma Productions.

The International Montessori Index. The Montessori "method" of bringing up and educating children. Montessori. Accessed February 15, 2014 from http://www.montessori.edu/, 2014.

Johnson, M., & Heller, P. (Producers), & Famuyiwa, R. (Director). (2002). *Brown Sugar* [Motion Picture]. United States: Twentieth Century Fox Film Corporation.

Knight, G. R. (2008). *Issues & alternatives in educational philosophy* (4th ed.). Berrien Springs, MI: Andrews University Press.

Leslie-Toogood, Adrienne. "Introduction." In *Advising Student-Athletes: A Collaborative Approach to Success*, edited by Adrienne Leslie-Toogood and Emmett Gill, 7-12. Manhattan, KS: National Academic Advising Association, 2008.

Marcia, J. E. (1966). Development and validation of ego identity status. *Journal of Personality and Social Psychology, 21*, 551-559.

McLeod, S. (2018). Jean Piaget's Theory of Cognitive Development, Retrieved from https://www.simplypsychology.org/piaget.html

Miller, G. (2012). *Jerry Miller Memorial Greg and Michelle Miller.* Retrieved from https://www.youtube.com/watch?v=XZMM1zUc9us

Miller, G. (2012). *Jerry Miller Memorial Part 2 Mr. Hanberg.* Retrieved from https://www.youtube.com/watch?v=onjgcJBJJ6c

Miller, R. (2002). *Free schools, free people: Education and democracy after the 1960's.* New

York, NY: State University of New York Press.

Park, Andrew. *The Holy Spirit DMin Intensive Presentation.* Accessed March 19, 2014, http://online.united.edu/, January 28, 2014.

Peace, Richard. *Spiritual Autobiography, Discovering and Sharing Your Spiritual Story.* Colorado Springs, CO: NavPress, 1998.

Peters, George W. *A Biblical Theology of Missions.* Chicago, IL: Moody Press, 1984.

Piaget, J. (1972). Intellectual evolution from adolescence to adulthood. *Human Development, 15*, 1-12.

Ratts, M. J., Singh, A. A., Nassar-McMillan, S., Butler, S. K., & McCullough, J. R. (2015). *Multicultural and social justice counseling competencies.* Retrieved from https://www.counseling.org/docs/default-source/competencies/multicultural-and-social-justice-counseling-competencies.pdf?sfvrsn=8573422c_20

Robinson-Wood, T. (2017). *The Convergence of Race, Ethnicity, and Gender: Multiple identities in counseling* (5th ed). Thousand Oaks, CA: SAGE Publishing.

Rumbold, B. (n.d.). *Pastoral Care, The Pastoral Care Council of the ACT.* Retrieved from http://www.pastoralcareact.org/what-is-pastoral-care/

Sailes, Gary, and Louis Harrison. "Social Issues of Sport." In *Advising Student-Athletes: A Collaborative Approach to Success,* edited by Adrienne

Leslie-Toogood and Emmett Gill, 13-22. Manhattan, KS: National Academic Advising Association, 2008.

Sporting Charts. (2015). *Sporting Charts explains halftime.* Retrieved from https://www.sportingcharts.com/dictionary/nba/halftime.aspx.

Stanley, C. F. (2017). *Finding God's blessings in brokenness: How pain reveals his deepest love.* Grand Rapids, MI: Zondervan.

Stryer, B. K., Tofler, I. R., & Lapchick, R. (1998). A developmental overview of child and youth sports in society. *Sports Psychiatry, 7,* 697-724.

Valentine, J. J., & Taub, D. J. (1999). Responding to the developmental needs of student athletes. *Journal of College Counseling, 21,* 164-179.

Whitfield, Norman; and Barrett Strong. *Papa Was a Rollin' Stone.* Detroit, MI: Hittsville USA, 1972.

Wimberly, Edward, P. *Counseling African-American Marriages and Families.* Louisville, KY: Westminster John Knox Press, 1997.

Wimberly, Edward, P. *Counseling African American Marriages and Families.* Louisville, KY: Westminster John Knox Press, 1997.

ABOUT THE AUTHOR

Taunya Marie Tinsley, D.Min., Ph.D., NCC, LPC, graduated in December 2005 from Duquesne University with a Ph.D. in Counselor Education and Supervision. She received her M.A. degree in Higher Education Administration and College Student Development in 1995 from the University of Iowa. Dr. Tinsley also holds a B.A. in Business Administration from Augsburg College in Minneapolis, MN where she was also inducted in the Athletic Hall of Fame in September 2014. In April 2013, Dr. Tinsley completed her requirements for the Certificate in Missional Theology from Biblical Theological Seminary. Finally, in December 2016 Dr. Tinsley earned her Doctor of Ministry with a focus in Prophetic Congregational Development Using 21st Century Methods, Establishing Strong Leadership from United Theological Seminary in Dayton, OH.

Dr. Tinsley has a wealth of experience providing appropriate personal and academic growth opportunities for those seeking to become professional master's degree-level counselors as well as for those helping professionals seeking advanced or specialty areas of training and development in multicultural education and counseling, spiritual and Christian interventions, and sports counseling/athlete development. Dr. Tinsley spent nine years at California University of Pennsylvania as an Associate Professor in the Department of Counselor Education and Program Coordinator for the Sports Counseling Certificate Program. Dr. Tinsley has also served as the Director of Graduate Programs in Counseling at both Waynesburg University and Missio Seminary. In the fall 2019, Dr. Tinsley will begin a new journey as an Assistant Professor in the Education and Counseling Department at Villanova University.

In addition to providing academic and administrative services, Dr. Tinsley is the Owner of Transitions Counseling Service LLC and Life Skills Program that includes a ministry division, Love and Basketball Ministries, where she provides individual, marriage, family and group counseling and consultative services. Additionally, Dr. Tinsley is a facilitator with the New Paradigm Ministries Leadership Training as part of the Ephesus Project and is the Clinical Director of the Mount Ararat Baptist Church Counseling Center both in Pittsburgh, PA.

Dr. Tinsley has also managed to stay active in both the workplace and in the community advocating for and promoting organizations, helping professionals, and their clients. She has served as the North Atlantic Regional Representative for the Association for Multicultural Counseling and Development (AMCD), the President of the Pennsylvania College Counseling Association, and the President of the Pennsylvania Counseling Association. In 2006, Dr. Tinsley collaborated with the American Counseling Association to develop, facilitate, and enhance the Sports Counseling Interest Network. Dr. Tinsley serves on the board for the Association of Spiritual, Ethical and Religious Values in Counseling (ASERVIC) as well as begin her term as AMCD President on July 1, 2019.

Dr. Tinsley's interdisciplinary areas of counseling, research, and publications include multicultural issues in counseling, multicultural training and organizational development, spiritual and Christian interventions in counseling, sports counseling, and youth, adolescent, and adult development through sports.